The simple joy and honesty of this book lends a clear and practiced voice to a much-needed conversation—one regarding the global importance of ruralness and the cultures that exist and evolve there.

Timothy Charles, Chef, The Fogo Island Inn

I've had the pleasure of working with Lori McCarthy for several years now, both for my podcast and TV show, WildFed. From the moment I arrived in Newfoundland, she made sure I was immersed in the culture—the people, the places, the colours, textures, sights, smells, and, of course, the flavours. As someone who fishes the waters, hunts the land, foragers the diverse terrain, and accumulates the stories, Lori is uniquely qualified to write about the food, culture, history, and lore of Newfoundland.

Daniel Vitalis, *WildFed*

This book, like its author, is a Newfoundland treasure. Lori is spearheading a rejuvenation by reminding us of the bounties of our land, sea, and soil, and knitting together long-cherished family recipes and traditional knowledge with modern twists. Lori opens our eyes to the food potential that surrounds us, and the mouth-watering ways we can enjoy and appreciate the same resources that have sustained and enriched Newfoundland families for generations.

Jen Shears, Natural Boutique

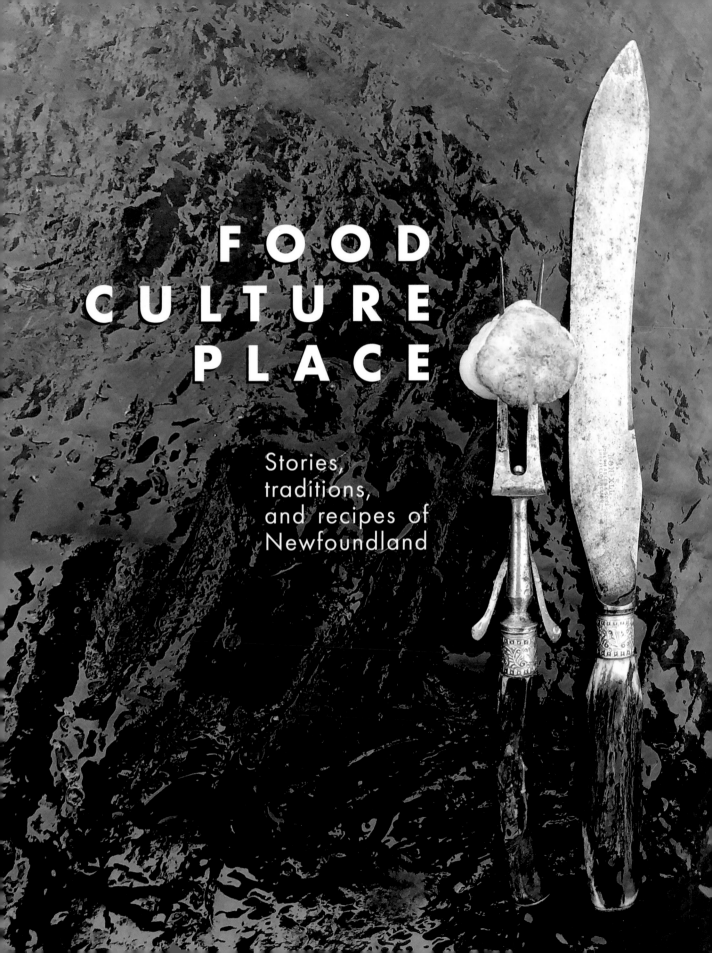

FOOD CULTURE PLACE

Stories,
traditions,
and recipes of
Newfoundland

Sunrise, Adies Lake

Library and Archives Canada Cataloguing in Publication

Title: Food, culture, place : stories, traditions, and recipes of Newfoundland / Lori McCarthy &
    Marsha Tulk.
Names: McCarthy, Lori, author. | Tulk, Marsha, author.
Description: Includes bibliographical references and index.
Identifiers: Canadiana 20210282916 | ISBN 9781989417317 (hardcover)
Subjects: LCSH: Cooking, Canadian—Newfoundland and Labrador style. | LCSH: Diet—Newfoundland and
    Labrador. | LCGFT: Cookbooks.
Classification: LCC TX715.6 .M33 2021 | DDC 641.59718,Äîdc23

Published by Boulder Books
Portugal Cove-St. Philip's, Newfoundland and Labrador
www.boulderbooks.ca

Design and layout: Todd Manning
Editor: Stephanie Porter
Copy editor: Iona Bulgin
Cover design: Tanya Montini
Cover photos: Marsha Tulk (front); Ritche Perez (back)
Front cover painting: G. Scott MacLeod, www.macleod9.com
Plate on front cover: Alexis Templeton, www.alexistempletonstudio.com

Printed in China

We acknowledge the financial support of the Government of Newfoundland and
Labrador through the Department of Tourism, Culture, Arts and Recreation.

Funded by the   Financé par le
Government   gouvernement
of Canada   du Canada   Canada

FOOD CULTURE PLACE

Stories, traditions, and recipes of Newfoundland

LORI MCCARTHY & MARSHA TULK

BOULDER BOOKS

CONTENTS

Author Forewords

In 2016, I reached out to my brother Andrew, a designer and artist, and asked him to create an image built around the words *Food, Culture, Place*. I had no specific reason for my request, but I felt that these words embodied and encompassed my work, and I wanted to see them written as a reminder of what drives me to do what I do. I had no plans for them to become the title of a book—but here we are, and for that I am so grateful.

Lori McCarthy

The purpose of this book is to help keep the food and food traditions of Newfoundland part of our culture for generations to come. To share what so many people of this island have shared with me—their recipes, their kitchen tables, their stories of a daughter's first hunt or a son's first time setting a rabbit snare. My cup runneth over, thanks to everyone who sat with me and shared. This book is a way to capture who they are as people of this province—their voices, their love for this place, and their pride in a way of life.

Until I was about 30, I didn't pay attention to why we ate fresh rabbits only in the fall of the year and bottled rabbit in February. I did, however, know that my brother Darrell would go off and check his slips (rabbit snares) in the morning before school and Mom bottled rabbit to put up (store in the pantry) for the winter, but I never stopped to consider why. Why he wasn't checking slips in March or July, or why the rabbits were sometimes white and sometimes brown (brown in the summer to stay hidden against the brush and white in the fall to blend in with the snow).

I didn't know which hunting seasons were when or anything about quotas or regulations. I didn't know that slips were set on "rabbit runs" and that you put little sticks under the snare to "show the rabbit the path of least resistance" (thank you, Jim McCarthy) along the path. I didn't know that rabbits love alder or that those rabbits were actually snowshoe hare or Arctic hare; the snowshoe hare was introduced to the island (by a parish priest, I'm told) as a food source. I just wasn't paying attention. Dad brought home fish all summer, Darrell snared rabbits, Bill brought home trout, Uncle Burt gave us moose, Mom cooked, and I ate.

But now I notice the ground beneath my feet, which way the wind blows, what grows in the lun (the sheltered side), and why some bays have mussels and some don't. I pay attention to the sharp bitten edge of an alder branch, the south-facing side of a hill full of mushrooms, the beautiful why and how of the bounty that lives all around me.

The stories of who we are and how we persevered against all odds can be seen in the way we harvest, cultivate, store, preserve, and prepare our food for the table. These traditions tie together our past, present, and future and tell the story of food, culture, and place.

• • •

As you read this book, I hope you see the labour of love the food of Newfoundland is for me and for all of us. I hope you appreciate the story of who we are and how we thrive on this land, on its waterways and on the sea—and how magical it is. I hope that you find inspiration from what I have learned and maybe discover a new appreciation for some of these foods yourself that you can then pass on to others. For readers who are not from Newfoundland, I hope this book inspires you to dive deep into your own food culture.

My journey has just begun. I have connected deeply to my place through its foods and now have an unwavering commitment to pay attention. To listen when Marsha's dad, Bill, shares his knowledge of the salmon on the mighty Humber River; when Roy Dwyer from Tilting, Fogo Island, tells stories old and new of the seal hunt; when Jer-

Lori and her father, Bill Butler.

emiah and Angie sit with me and share recipes of dark Christmas cake and stories of their son's first hunt. When Larry Hann takes me cod jiggin' and teaches me how to know where to drop the line, how to tell where the ocean floor drops off, based on nothing but landmarks, and when he shares with me how smart the geese are and what it takes to bag one.

Maybe you have heard many of these types of stories before and know all about plucking a turr, landing a salmon, and deboning and rolling a rabbit—or maybe you haven't. Either way, maybe you will enjoy them as much as I have enjoyed collecting them and sharing them with you.

I believe our food holds up to the best of the best. I believe it is the soul of who we are. Our perseverance, our wisdom, and our love of the land and sea make us who we are today. To all Newfoundlanders out there reading this, this book is my praise for and my pride in this island, its people, and its food. I hope we have done you proud.

ON BEING FROM NEWFOUNDLAND AND BEING FROM LABRADOR

I want to say a few words about why this book has been called *Food, Culture, Place: Stories, Traditions, and Recipes of Newfoundland* and not *Newfoundland and Labrador*. The province of Newfoundland and Labrador is divided into two landmasses: the island portion of the province and that attached to the continent of North America bordering Québec.

Those of us who grew up on the island portion say we're from Newfoundland, those who grew up in Labrador would say that they grew up in Labrador or that they're from the Big Land. And it is a majestic big land indeed; one that I have only been blessed enough to plant my feet on once.

I cannot wait for the day when I get to travel to Labrador to capture its stories, recipes, and the food culture, but until then I will share what I have learned and gathered from the island of Newfoundland.

Lori McCarthy

Lori and Vanessa Kenny.

Marsha and her mom,
Linda Hudson.

I grew up in Pasadena on the west coast of New-foundland. We'd take frequent trips to my paternal grandparents' house—the Hudson family home. It was a two-storey white clapboard farmhouse, with a root cellar and workshop in the basement, an attached pantry room and porch on the back, and a weird little windowless room on the second floor that I knew only as the dark room. There were so many spaces to explore both inside and out, but the best was this dark room.

Marsha Tulk

My grandfather was a collector of things. He would gather them, put similar items together in recycled boxes, label the boxes with a wax pencil, and place them on the narrow shelves that went from floor to ceiling in that room.

Later in life, I found out that this dark room was actually a photographic darkroom. In one of the labelled boxes on those shelves were hundreds of medium-format negatives and contact printed photographs in recycled Kodak photopaper boxes. These photographs were taken by my grandfather; he would process the film and make the prints in the windowless room. I even found his cameras and the processing trays.

My grandfather's photographs consistently popped up in my work for a Fine Arts degree in photography at Grenfell College. To this day, I still carve out time to scan and catalogue these photos and blast my father and mother with questions about the who, what, and where that are contained in the images. This book has been the first opportunity since my college days to showcase these cultural images. And to place them in the context of traditional foods is exciting.

I love to cook. For a long time, I didn't think too deeply about food or my perspective on it. I try to make things from scratch as much as possible. I strive to know where my food comes from and if I can source it locally myself, I probably will. I didn't think to applaud "traditional" ingredients as special or unique. They are just what I have always had.

I do know that Newfoundland's food culture cannot be defined by one ingredient. Cod is not king in many areas, and I am constantly surprised by the variety of regional ingredients the people of this island have survived on.

I like knowing what time of year it is, not by the calendar but by what is being caught, hunted, planted, picked, or preserved—this is the premise of this book. Being on an island with its share of sustainability hurdles makes this concept even more important.

I like that obtaining fresh food gets you outdoors. Being outside not only connects you with the food you are gathering but also the people you are with while doing it. It makes you aware of and appreciate where food comes from, how it survives in this environment, and how best to preserve it for the future. The biology of food, where it lives, what it ate, and how it interacts with its surroundings is fascinating. If you are alone, you connect with yourself and how you affect the things around you and sometimes how hard it is to get the things you want to your plate.

I like how food gathers people together. It can be as simple as a boil-up out in the country or family and friends gathering for occasions, be it happy or sad. Food is a large part of the bond I have with my family—not just connecting around the table but also during the process of making. The first question of the day, now a bit of a reoccurring joke, is "What are we taking out for supper?" With that you walk down the stairs to the freezer or to the pantry to take out what you need. Then you think about what other ingredients you need and how you are going to prepare it.

I like how talking about food brings people out of the woodwork. I wouldn't have met Lori if it were not for a discussion about creating "our" food. She has expanded the way I think about our "everyday" ingredients. I now search out people just to talk about one particular recipe from their region. And usually, before we are finished chatting, I have sampled a meal's worth of food, recorded more than half a dozen recipes, been given an armful of goods to take with me, and received a future invite for supper. My greatest realization is that traditional processes are not difficult or complicated, but precise. Food is prepared with care and pride. This is why the traditions have survived, and why we need to continue its survival.

•••

My main work in putting together this book was developing and photographing recipes, but my overall goal was to create content that tells a story.

This book has been a journey through the 32,552 photos I have collected over the years. But I wouldn't delete a single one. I have spent countless hours scanning my family's collections of negatives, slides, and prints. Even more hours went into cooking the food we feature in this book, trying to take the perfect shot, then celebrating by eating all of what we had made. I'm not sure what was the best part.

In the process of making this book, I was amazing by the similarities between the generations of our families. Many of our family activities were similar—from picnics to salmon fishing to harvesting and preserving—and, the best part, over three (sometimes four) generations, we all documented these activities. My generation most often documents digitally. The generation before me dropped off whole rolls of film and received stacks of 4 x 6 glossy colour prints or small boxes of cardboard-framed slides. The generation before that made beautiful black and white contact prints from medium-format negatives, the format I loved best while in art school. But we all wanted to keep memories alive and to hopefully pass them on.

It is said that a picture tells a thousand words. Putting food, culture, and place together has the potential to tell a thousand stories. By making the food, looking at the photographs, and reading the stories in this book, we hope your own personal stories will come to the surface, no matter where you are from.

Marsha Tulk

HOW WE ORGANIZED THIS BOOK

Deeply entwined with the seasons and connected to the land and sea, the foods and recipes of Newfoundland follow a way of eating throughout the year. We have tried to emulate this in the organization of this book.

We begin in April, May, and June, just as the ground begins to come alive after a long, cold winter.

The bounty from the land and sea is highlighted in the season that it can be hunted, harvested, and fished. The recipes in each section reflect how foods that come into season can be enjoyed fresh and put right on your plate—and how to pickle, preserve, and prepare for later in the year. This is how many people still eat on this island. Hunt, fish, harvest, smoke, salt, bottle, and preserve it when it's in season to be enjoyed and treasured later.

As an example, in July / August / September, you'll find a recipe for halibut tacos—best made with fresh fish—but also a recipe for smoked halibut that can be put up for the winter so you can enjoy smoked halibut pasta in January. You'll see a rabbit roulade in January / February / March made with a fresh whole rabbit, as well as a brining and bottling process so that rabbit can be enjoyed later in the woods or on a fishing trip. The whole book is laid out like this.

In the back of the book, you'll find a list of plants that were foraged for these recipes. A photo index offers information about the people and places where much of the food we've written about was enjoyed and processed.

These photos have a place in our hearts and share the story of this place. We encourage you to gather stories, recipes, and photos and share them with your children, your family, and the world because they matter to your culture and to those coming up behind us.

A NOTE ON MEASURES

Most measurements in this book are given in cups, teaspoons, tablespoons and imperial units—this is how most of the recipes were given to us. For certain recipes, specifically those that involve curing meat, metric equivalents are provided. Curing meat requires precision, and we find the best way to ensure accurate quantities is by using weight, most commonly grams.

after the long haul

APRIL

MAY

JUNE

"When you go bottling and canning, make the one big mess then you're good for the year."

–Shirley Butler, Pouch Cove

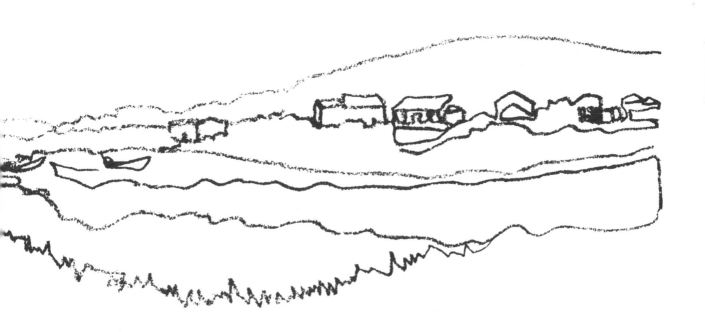

The Capelin Roll

The capelin roll in Newfoundland is a delight. I live in a small community on the edge of the capital of Newfoundland. Every year, my younger son and I make at least one walk from our house to Middle Cove beach with our salt meat buckets and cast net in hand to catch a few capelin.

In late June or early July, large schools of capelin—a small silver-bellied fish with an iridescent green-and-black back—make their way from the north to the sandy shores, coves, and inlets of Newfoundland to spawn. As my son and I head down the hill toward the coming high tide, we pass long lines of cars parked along the side of the road. We approach the beach parking lot, part of a wave of people on their annual pilgrimage to where the water meets the smooth, surf-tumbled rocks. Parents, grandparents, and friends are heavily laden with buckets and boots and blankets, trying to keep a watchful eye on their children who are frantically waving around their new dip nets.

The closer you get to the beach, the stronger the smell of wood smoke from the campfires dotted along the crescent of the cove. You'll hear a multitude of dialects; these small silver creatures bring together many nationalities. As the swarm of fish gets closer to the shore, everyone has a chance to fill their buckets, bags, and coolers. Those who cannot wade in to get their own won't go home empty-handed; more than enough nets are dipped and thrown to catch several meals. Children squeal as the capelin that escape desperately wriggle toward the water's edge. These waves of people continue all day and into the night, much like the fish they chase. The haze of the wood smoke at night fills the cove like that of the early morning fog. From the Middle Cove lookout, I counted over 30 fires in one night.

When my sons were younger, they sold firewood at the beach as a summer job to make some pocket money. One year my younger son decided to write his heritage fair project about the capelin roll. We found one of the few remaining cast-net makers, Eric Dodge from Conception Bay South, to make him his own net for that season. As a very young boy, Mr. Dodge had learned how to weave nets from his father. There were never written instructions—you learned by watching and doing. We still use that net.

My parents took my brother and me to Middle Cove to see the capelin roll when we were young. My husband and I have carried our children on our backs and held their hands as they waded into the waves of little fishes. Now that my children are older, they help me cast the net and carry the filled buckets. They help fill the buckets of others when ours are full. I hope the capelin stocks are maintained for future generations. I hope my children continue to go and bring others with them to witness it. Let's keep those beach fires glowing late into the night. **MT**

CAPELIN CAKES

While looking at Instagram reels one day, I came across a Turkish fishmonger and chef who made interesting and quick fish dishes. I'm not sure what fish he was using for one fried fish dish, but it resembled our capelin. It was a fish cake, but the deboned fish were wrapped around a stuffing and pan-fried. Capelin season was upon us and I had to make a Newfoundland version. The chef looked to be using spinach in the stuffing—it also happened to be the time of year for the fresh turnip greens. To add a little more traditional flavour, I decided to include parsnips.

This recipe works well with freshly caught capelin in the spring but also smelts in the winter. Smelts will make a slightly larger cake. If fresh greens are not readily available, go a little Turkish and use spinach instead.

---

36 capelin

1 large white onion, finely diced

1 lb fresh turnip greens, cleaned and finely chopped

2 parsnips, peeled and finely grated

Salt and pepper

2 cups fine cornmeal

Canola oil

1 lemon

To prepare the capelin, cut off the head and tail. Cut open the belly from head to tail to remove the gut. Press open, grasp the spine at the head end, and gently remove. It should pull away from the body of the fish fairly easily, especially if the fish are fresh.

Mix the onion, greens, and parsnip together in a bowl. Season with salt and pepper.

Generously sprinkle cornmeal over a small teacup saucer. Lay 6 capelin, skin side down, in a star pattern, with tails slightly overlapping in the centre and the heads hanging over the edge of the saucer. Spoon a heaping tablespoon of the onion mixture in the centre of the capelin fillets. Fold the ends of the fillets over onto the filling. Generously dust with more cornmeal and gently turn the fish cake onto your hand. Press gently to make the cake firm and place to one side. Do the same with the remaining capelin. You should have 6 cakes. Heat the oil in a large skillet over medium heat. Gently place the cakes in the skillet and fry until golden brown. Flip each cake and continue frying on the other side until golden brown. Plate and squeeze a little fresh lemon juice on top. **MT**

BOTTLED CAPELIN

My father introduced me to Clayton and Madeline Watkins at their cabin on Flat Bay River on the west coast of Newfoundland, where my parents also have a cabin. Clayton is originally from Summerford, Notre Dame Bay, and Madeline is from Bridgeport, also on Notre Dame Bay. Clayton had given my father a bottle of dried capelin—neither my father or I had ever seen capelin preserved like that. While visiting my parents at their cabin this past summer, I convinced my father to take me down the lane to meet Clayton and hopefully learn his recipe and technique.

Clayton processes 26 bottles of capelin at a time in two pots with two layers of bottles in each. He says that frying all of his capelin took such a long time that he needed to find a quicker method. While canning his capelin one year, he came up with the answer—deep-frying. He has been deep-frying his capelin for 2 minutes in canola oil ever since. **MT**

Fresh capelin

Salt

Canola oil

Prepare a quantity of basic salt brine, enough to completely cover the amount of capelin you are bottling. Use the floating potato method to determine the amount of salt to add (combine salt and water; once a medium potato starts to float in the brine, you have added enough salt). Place rinsed fresh capelin in the brine for exactly 3 minutes. Use a dip net to remove the capelin. Lay all the capelin out on a shrimp net or other fine netting. Lightly hose down the capelin. Dry them for a few days in the shade, keeping the flies off with fine mesh netting. After drying, the capelin can be frozen if needed.

When you are ready to bottle, cut off the capelin heads and discard. Fry the bodies in canola oil for 1 minute per side. Lay the fried capelin on paper towel to drain. Pack approximately 22 to 24 capelin in each sterilized 500-millilitre bottle. Simmer the filled bottles in a water bath for 1½ hours.

Recipe by Clayton Watkins

Hauling a cod trap, St. George's Bay.

HERRING CEVICHE

To make juniper salt, combine ¼ cup of juniper berries with ¼ cup of regular salt using a mortar and pestle or blender. If you don't have access to juniper, substitute with salt of your choice.

1 fresh herring

4 to 6 limes

½ tsp juniper salt

2 green onions, chopped

1 green apple, diced

1 bunch fresh lovage, chopped (fresh cilantro or coriander can be substituted)

1 sweet red or yellow pepper, diced

1 jalapeno pepper, seeded and diced

Fillet and skin the herring. Cut the fillets lengthwise in half, then chop into small cubes. Place the chopped herring in a bowl. You don't need to de-bone the herring; the lime juice dissolves the bones. Add the zest of 1 lime, plus enough juice to cover or nearly cover the herring. Add the salt and onion to the herring and stir. Allow the herring to "cook" in the lime juice for 3 hours; if it is not completely submerged in the lime juice, stir every 30 to 40 minutes while marinating. Add the apple, pepper, jalapeno, and fresh herbs just before serving.

If you are taking this on a boil-up or picnic, layer the marinated herring in the bottom of a container, with the apple, peppers, and fresh herbs on top. Leave stirring room on the top to prevent the apple and peppers from going soft. When you arrive at your destination, mix and enjoy. **MT**

COLD SMOKED HERRING

I like to add crushed juniper berries, whole peppercorns, bay leaves, and coriander seeds to this brine—you can add aromatics to suit your preference.

This brine recipe is also used for hot smoked halibut.

6 fresh herring, filleted from the back not the belly

BRINE

70 g (4 tbsp) sea salt

30 g (2 tbsp + ½ tsp) brown sugar

500 ml (2 cups) water

1 tsp juniper berries

1 tsp peppercorns

8 bay leaves

1 tsp coriander

The above ingredients will make enough brine for 6 herring fillets, but the brine can easily be multiplied. As my smoker easily holds 12 fillets, I double the brine.

Mix all the ingredients in a nonreactive container until most of the salt and sugar has been dissolved. Add the spices. Place the fillets in the brine for 45 minutes. At 45 minutes, remove the fillets from the brine, rinse, pat dry, and lay each fillet skin side down on the smoker's wire racks. Let them air-dry until completely dry to the touch. The drier the surface of the herring, the better the smoke will stick. Set up the smoker for a cold smoke with hardwood and smoke for 4 hours. Cool completely. Vacuum-seal each fillet and freeze for your next breakfast or boil-up. **MT**

HOT SMOKED HALIBUT

As for the herring recipe above, I like using crushed juniper berries, whole peppercorns, bay leaves, and coriander seeds.

1 fresh halibut steak

BRINE

70 g (4 tbsp) sea salt

30 g (2 tbsp + ½ tsp) brown sugar

500 ml (2 cups) water

Aromatics of your choice

Mix all ingredients in a nonreactive container until most of the salt and sugar has dissolved. Add the aromatics of your choice.

Place the fillets in the brine and soak 45 minutes. At 45 minutes, remove the fillets from the brine, rinse, pat dry, and lay each fillet skin side down on the smoker's wire racks. Air-dry until completely dry to the touch. Use hardwood and bring the smoker to a temperature between 220°F and 250°F. Hot-smoke for approximately 60 minutes or until the internal temperature reaches 140°F.

Eat the halibut immediately or completely cool, vacuum-pack, and freeze for later use. **MT**

The two recipes for smoked fish in this section of the book (Hot Smoked Halibut, page 20, and Cold Smoked Herring, page 19) require different smoking processes. In a hot smoke, the fish is not cured but is fully cooked as it smokes. A cold smoked fish, however, is cured prior to smoking and is exposed to heat for flavour, not to cook the fish.

	HOT SMOKE	COLD SMOKE
SMOKER TEMPERATURE	275°C to 300°C	< 86°C
SMOKING TIME	About one hour, depending on type of fish and thickness	Four to 12 hours, depending on type of fish and level of smoke preference

On Turrs

Larry Hann is a personality larger than life itself. "You'll find no better," as my mother would say. His passion for an early morning goose hunt—heading out the narrows of Quidi Vidi harbour in his boat at 5 a.m.—is beautifully woven into his passion for this island. A lovely, generous, intelligent man who loves a good story and a feed of fresh turrs.

It brings him more joy to share his harvest with those he knows will appreciate it than if he kept it for himself. I have come home many times to a few turrs hanging on my front door and received many a call from Larry saying, "Where ya to? I just stopped by with a feed of fresh fish. It's in the fridge in the garage." I thank him so much for sharing his knowledge, for his enthusiasm for this land, and for the food he has shared with me and my family—including the turrs that made this recipe.

One March day Larry called and said he was "going out at a few turrs in the shed" and asked if I wanted to help. He was just in off the water and wanted to clean them right away. I had previously asked him several times if he could show me how to pluck the birds, and I jumped at the opportunity.

I recorded some video of Larry as he plucked the bird.

He is holding the full feathered bird by the beak and the legs. A big boiler of rapidly boiling water is at the ready.

What am I doing? I'm dipping the turr, one, two, three, four.

In and out of the boiling water, he dips the bird four times. Holding it in for two or three seconds each dip. This helps the feathers release, but also renders the skin very delicate and susceptible to tearing.

Make sure the bird doesn't touch the sides of the pot; if it touches the pot you will tear the bird.

I now know the importance of that, after hours of plucking! If you tear the skin of the bird while plucking, the bird starts to release the heavy layer of fat beneath the skin. This oil makes plucking so much more difficult. ("You need a bottle of rum to spend the afternoon pickin'," my mom says.)

The bird comes out of the pot and onto a homemade table for picking birds. The tabletop is a piece of plywood, a little higher than hip-height; in the centre is a large hole with a bucket under it. A place to put all the feathers.

Now, what I'm doing ... He starts plucking from the legs up to the breast in an upward motion. *Starting up, up, up, up,* as he quickly takes off a little tuft of feathers, but not too many so he doesn't tear the skin.

Marsha struggled to come up with a new (acceptable) twist on turr; she made many attempts and many choice words were said. I serve turr in tacos, in ravioli, and—just like the recipe that follows—seared and sliced as a little taste with a beer. I also now have a new appreciation for roasted turr, smothered in gravy and eaten around my mom's table. After all, it's not what you eat but the people you enjoy it with. **LM**

A TASTE OF TURR

Growing up, the only way I had ever known a turr to be cooked was roasted almost to the point of incineration. Those turrs also had the rare ability to be a bird but taste like a fish. I was determined to find a way to cook a turr that I liked. Here it goes ...

2 deboned turr breasts

Salt and pepper

⅔ cup olive oil

⅓ cup Aquavit

12 juniper berries, crushed

Season the turr breasts on both sides with salt and pepper. Place the olive oil, Aquavit, and juniper berries in a bowl and stir well. Marinate the turr breasts in this mixture for 30 minutes. Reserve the leftover marinade.

Remove the turr breasts from the marinade and skewer each breast on a juniper twig. Quickly sear each breast in a hot cast-iron pan or on a barbeque for 1 minute per side. Place the cooked breasts back in the marinade to lightly recoat. Remove from the marinade, pull out the juniper skewer, and serve. **MT**

RICOTTA GNOCCHI

Making fresh ricotta is a simple process that only takes 30 minutes from start to finish. It is very versatile cheese that can be enjoyed in gnocchi or simply served up with crusty bread, drizzled with honey, and sprinkled with toasted nuts and fresh edible flowers.

1½ cups fresh ricotta cheese (see recipe page 30)

½ cup + 2 tbsp flour

1 egg

If you make homemade ricotta, which I recommend you do, let it hang for 15 to 20 minutes. Squeeze out the moisture while it is still in the hanging cheesecloth. If you use store-bought ricotta, you will want to hang it in cheesecloth to dry it out, and squeeze out the excess liquid. The goal is to have a dry crumbly cheese the texture of crumbled feta cheese.

Place a large pot of heavily salted water over high heat and bring to a boil. Cover and reduce to a simmer.

Lightly loosen the fresh ricotta into a pile with your fingers over a lightly floured clean surface. Sprinkle with ½ cup flour. Continue to mix and loosen the flour-cheese mixture with your fingers. Make a well in the centre and crack the egg into it. Lightly beat the egg with a fork and gradually mix into the surrounding ricotta-flour mixture. Do not overwork.

Combine all ingredients and gently knead, adding additional flour (approximately 2 tablespoons) as needed. Fold and knead about 20 times. The dough should be slightly springy but not sticky.

Using a scraper or a sharp knife, cut the dough into 6 equal pieces. Lightly dust each and roll into a slender log approximately ½ to 1 inch thick. Cut each log into 1-inch pieces. These pieces can be cooked immediately, or they can be pushed over a wooden gnocchi board or the back of a fork to form the signature ridged gnocchi texture.

Place the gnocchi in the simmering water and gently boil until they float to the surface. Remove from the water with a slotted spoon, place in a large serving bowl, and dress in your choice of sauce or toppings. **LM**

FRESH RICOTTA CHEESE

8 cups whole milk

¼ cup lemon juice, freshly squeezed

Pour the milk in a large heavy pot over medium heat and slowly bring to 180°F. Stir occasionally to prevent the milk from scorching. At 180°F, you will notice steam, little bubbles around the edge of the milk, and the formation of a film on the surface. It should take about 20 minutes to get to this point.

Reduce the heat to low and add the lemon juice. Slowly and gently stir the mixture for about 2 minutes. You will notice the milk curds (the ricotta) separating from the whey (the yellowish liquid). Remove from the heat, cover the pot, and let it stand 20 minutes.

Place a colander or strainer lined with cheesecloth (or a thin cotton towel) inside a large bowl. The cheesecloth must be large enough so that you can gather the edges over the cheese and tie together with string.

Carefully ladle the ricotta into the lined colander. Gather the edges of the cloth and tie tightly with a long piece of string. Make a loop in the tail of the string so that you can hang the cheese over the strainer and bowl. The knob of an upper cupboard door makes an ideal spot to hang the package. The consistency of the cheese depends on the amount of time you leave the ricotta to drain. For a dryer ricotta, which you need to make gnocchi, let it hang for up to 20 minutes.

Use immediately or put in an airtight container and refrigerate for later use. Don't discard the whey. This liquid is high in milk protein and can replace water in bread recipes; it makes a deliciously rich bread. **MT**

Fresh Flippers

Mom will often turn to me as she's cooking and say, "Now, that's not anything fancy like you would cook." She doesn't realize that the reason her food is so delicious is because she knows how to prepare foods properly, and how to put a taste on a rubber boot, I'm sure. She knows, just as a professional cook knows, about deglazing a pan and picking the right cut of meat for the dish she's preparing. She doesn't need a thermometer for it to turn out just right.

Generations of families have been preparing seal for the table, and she's learned from them: the flippers must be fresh, they must be kept on ice or at least very cold, they must be put into the sink and doused with baking soda and cleaned meticulously of fat. She knows that it's the fat that can turn rancid and, if not cared for properly, will give the dinner a horrible taste and stink up the house. I feel for anyone trying to sell Mom last year's flippers ("I knew the minute he took them out of the freezer and the fat was yellow that they were not this year's seal flippers, even though that's what he told me"). I'm sure she set him straight and left without the flippers.

I'm not sure the generation before me saw a need to change how foods like seal flipper are prepared. These were the simple, delicious meals that filled their bellies, prepared them for a day's work, or satisfied them after that day was done.

Nor am I sure how many of this next generation will continue to eat seal flipper pie. My hope is that they will, and they will continue to share the stories of the hunt and how it sustained so many families in this province. The work of people like Jen Shears (pictured on page 35) of the Natural Boutique—along with chefs like Todd Perrin of Mallard Cottage, Shaun Hussey of Chinched Bistro, and Jeremy Charles of Raymond's— is crucial in continuing to advocate for our hunting culture. I am very hopeful. **LM**

SEAL FLIPPER SUPPER WITH DOUGH BOYS

2 fresh seal flippers, meticulously cleaned of all fat

1 onion, chopped

¼ cup diced cured pork fat (fatback)

2 tbsp salted butter

2 tbsp canola oil

Flour for dusting the flippers

½ tsp salt

½ tsp pepper

½ cup red wine

1 cup cubed carrot

1 cup cubed turnip

1 cup cubed potato

2-3 cups moose or beef broth, or water

In a frying pan, sautée the onion and pork fat on a low-medium heat until browned. Remove and reserve the onion and fat pieces. Lightly flour the seal flippers and fry in frying pan the rendered-out fat. If required, add a little butter and oil to your pan, just enough to brown the flippers on all sides. Deglaze the pan with red wine. Place the flippers, fried onion, and fatback in a roasting pan and pour over the red wine. Salt and pepper all over. Cover tightly.

Cook at 350°F for 1½ hours. Remove from the oven, add the cubed vegetables and enough broth or water to cover the vegetables by 2 inches. Cover and bake for another hour.

If you'd like a thicker gravy, thicken with a flour-water slurry. Serve with dough boys.

Dough Boys (Dumplings)
2 cups flour
2 tbsp baking powder
½ cup salted butter, softened
1 cup water
½ tsp pepper

Jen Shears, Natural Boutique.

Mix the flour, baking powder, and pepper in a bowl. Using your hands, combine the butter with the flour mixture until it sticks together when you squeeze it. The butter should be spread uniformly throughout.

Slowly add the water, while stirring as best you can, until the mixture has a doughy consistency. You don't want it too wet. Form the dough into balls a little bigger than a golf ball. (This recipe makes between eight and 10 balls depending on how big you make them.)

Place the roaster of seal stew on top of the stove and bring to a boil; drop in dough boys. Cover. Bring back to a boil and then simmer for 8 to 10 minutes. By then the dough boys will have doubled in size and will seem wet on the outside but nice and fluffy on the inside. Serve a dough boy or two per bowl. **LM**

BARLEY STUFFED SQUID

The place to find out about squid and all the ways to prepare it is on the Baie Verte peninsula, at least according to acquaintances of my parents. Baie Verte is located on the northwest coast of Newfoundland. Favourite preparations include cured dried squid, which can be toasted over an open fire, peeled, and then rubbed between your hands while still warm to shred enough to eat. There are also bottled squid rings and a wonderful thing called "sqwieners"—a bottle of pickled squid tubes, each stuffed with a wiener!

Stuffed squid is traditionally made with a bread dressing. This version is stuffed with a risotto, using pearl barley instead of rice. This is an opportunity to use up those sautéed frozen chanterelles you have been hoarding in your freezer all winter before you head out to pick fresh ones.

4 to 6 whole squid tubes, cleaned

4 cups beef broth

2 tbsp butter

1 small onion, minced

2 cloves garlic, minced

½ lb fresh or ½ cup cooked mushrooms

¼ tsp thyme

Freshly ground pepper

1 cup pearl barley

½ cup white wine

½ cup grated Parmesan cheese

Olive oil

½ cup salt pork, cut in small cubes

Preheat oven to 400°F. Heat the beef broth in a saucepan and keep warm. In a large, deep skillet, heat the butter over medium heat. Sauté the onion and garlic until softened. Add the mushrooms and thyme. Season with pepper. Cook, stirring, until the mushrooms are tender and golden. Add the barley and cook, stirring constantly for about 1 minute until the barley pearls are well coated and toasted.

Add the wine and cook, stirring, until all the wine has been absorbed. Add 1 ladleful of hot beef broth and stir to combine. Cook over medium heat, simmering gently and continually stirring until nearly all the broth has been absorbed. Continue adding ladlefuls of hot broth, one at a time, allowing each ladleful to be almost fully absorbed before adding another. Cook until all the broth is used. Test the barley to make sure it is al dente. If it is not, add another ladleful of hot broth and cook longer. Finish by stirring in the Parmesan cheese. Put the barley risotto to one side to slightly cool.

Fill each squid body with 2 to 3 tablespoons filling. Do not overfill the tubes or they will burst during baking. You may have leftover stuffing. Close the tube by pinning it together with a toothpick, using a weaving motion. Grease a 9 by 13-inch baking dish with olive oil. Lay the stuffed squid in the dish in one layer. Sprinkle any remaining stuffing over the squid. Pour ½ cup water into the dish, drizzle with more olive oil, and season with salt and pepper. Cover the dish tightly with foil and bake until the squid are cooked through, about 25 minutes.

Meanwhile, place the pork cubes in a small frying pan and fry until all of the fat is rendered out and the pieces are crispy. Strain the scrunchions (pieces of fried fat), place in a small bowl, and set aside. Check the squid for doneness. If the squid are cooked through, remove the foil, return the dish to the oven, and continue to bake until the tubes are golden on top. Top with the fried scrunchions and serve immediately. **MT**

Canning Lobster

The photograph on page 2 is of Percy Morris, sitting on his father's (Phillip Morris) stagehead on the beach of St. George's Bay. Percy is wiping the outside of a tin can. Inside the can is probably lobster meat. Lobster and salmon, along with herring, were the predominant fisheries in this area. The herring were caught in the spring and packed in wooden barrels made during the winter. Lobster and salmon were canned, sold, and shipped to merchant distributors to be labelled and resold to the market. The Morrises sold their cans to McFetridge's or Captain Bill Bennett on Skipper Sam's schooner to be shipped to Halifax, Nova Scotia, or Boston. In later years, some may have been put on the train headed to St. John's.

The process of canning was labour-intensive. After the product was put in the can, it was sealed and placed in a vat of boiling water for the prescribed amount of time. While the cans were still hot and expanded, a small hole was punched in its top to let the excess air escape. In addition to the air, fat and debris were expelled from the can. This had to be thoroughly cleaned off in order for the solder used to seal up the hole to stick. This process of wiping and soldering would sometimes have to be done several times on one can, since the solder would not stick if traces of fat remained.

39

LOBSTER BISQUE

This recipe can be made with freshly cooked lobsters, leftover fresh lobsters, or bottled, canned, or frozen lobster meat. It's one of those recipes that you can make with whatever is available. Plus, the broth is tasty enough that if someone is not that fussy about lobster, you can omit the meat. Just be warned: it's garlicy and spicy!

BROTH

2 tbsp butter

1 tbsp olive oil

1 onion, chopped

2 carrots, peeled and chopped

2 stalks celery, chopped

½ tsp fresh thyme

½ tsp fresh sweet gale (optional)

1 tsp concentrated bouillon powder

¼ tsp black pepper

¼ to ½ tsp cayenne pepper

4 cloves garlic, minced

2 tbsp tomato paste

3 tbsp all-purpose flour

1 cup white wine

4½ cups good-quality lobster, seafood, or chicken stock

¾ to 1 cup whipping cream

Heat the butter and oil in a large, heavy-bottomed pot over medium heat. When the butter has melted, add the onions, carrots, celery, and herbs and cook until soft. Season with the bouillon powder, black pepper, and cayenne pepper. Stir in the garlic and cook until fragrant. Mix in the tomato paste and cook for a minute to coat the vegetables. Sprinkle the flour over the vegetables and stir while cooking for another minute. Pour in the wine and stir. It will thicken immediately. Stir in the stock, reduce the heat, and gently bring to a simmer.

To add extra flavour to the stock, and if you have large pieces of shell available, add them at this point to simmer with the broth. After 30 minutes, turn off the heat and remove and discard the lobster shells. Blend the mixture with an immersion or countertop blender in small batches. Return the mixture to medium-low heat and stir in the whipping cream.

Melt the butter in a small saucepan over medium heat. Add the garlic and sauté until fragrant. Add the lobster meat; season with salt, pepper, and cayenne pepper to taste. Sauté for an additional minute until the meat is just warmed through.

To serve, pour the bisque into individual serving bowls and top each with the lobster meat and a drizzle of olive oil. **MT**

LOBSTER SHELLS

Legs and large pieces of shell from the cooked lobster, optional

GARLIC LOBSTER MEAT

1 cup lobster meat, cooked, from approximately
2 lobsters, whole pieces or roughly chopped

2 tbsp butter

2 cloves garlic, minced

Salt, pepper, and cayenne pepper to taste

STEAMED PARTRIDGEBERRY PUDDING

I remember so well coming home from church to the pot boiling on the stove and Sunday Jiggs' dinner almost ready. Vegetables—*yuck*. But there was also the most delicious pudding being boiled with the vegetables. I was the oldest of 14 children and, considering the crowd that was waiting for dessert, there was always a mad rush to finish the vegetables and be first for the pudding. To this day, this recipe is my go-to, especially when we have a crowd to feed. Never has it not been a hit. This recipe can be made with blueberries, cranberries, or any other berries, or even with raisins, or just plain.

½ cup salted butter, melted

½ cup brown sugar

½ cup molasses

½ cup hot water

1 tsp baking soda

1 tsp cinnamon

1½ cups all-purpose flour

2 cups partridgeberries, fresh or frozen

HOT SAUCE

½ cup salted butter, melted

1 cup brown sugar

1 tsp vanilla

2 cups boiling water

1 to 2 tsp custard powder

In a small bowl, mix the butter, brown sugar, and molasses with a spoon until smooth. In a large bowl, dissolve the baking soda in the hot water. Add the molasses mixture and stir until combined. Add the cinnamon and flour and mix well. Fold in the berries.

Grease a 4-cup pudding mould. Pour the batter into the mould and cover with the lid. Place the mould in a large pot filled with approximately 2 cups boiling water. Cover the pot and let the pudding simmer for 2½ hours. Add more water if needed so that the pot does not boil dry. Remove the pudding and let cool for 30 minutes. Remove from the mould.

In a small saucepan, mix together the butter, brown sugar, vanilla, and boiling water. Simmer on low and whisk until all the sugar has dissolved. Add custard powder while whisking continuously. Add enough to thicken the sauce as desired.

Slice the pudding into wedges and serve immediately with the hot sauce.

Recipe by Linda Hudson

SWEET POTATO CINNAMON KNOTS
WITH CANDIED CHANTERELLES

I t's time to break out those beautiful earthy chanterelles that you lovingly dehydrated in the fall. Candied chanterelles can be used in many ways in sweet or savoury dishes. And as a bonus, the syrup is delicious on pancakes or waffles instead of maple syrup.

CANDIED CHANTERELLES

2 cups water

1 cup white sugar +
up to 1 additional cup

1 tbsp vanilla

5 tsp dried chanterelles

CINNAMON BUNS

1 large sweet potato,
peeled and cubed

1 cup milk

½ cup salted butter

2 eggs

4½ cups all-purpose flour

1 tsp white sugar

2 tsp dry active yeast

Make the candied chanterelles ahead of time. Break large mushrooms into pieces; smaller pieces will have more of a candied taste.

Bring the water and 1 cup sugar to a low simmer until the sugar has dissolved. Add the chanterelles. Simmer until the liquid is reduced by half, about 10 minutes. Add the vanilla and another ½ to 1 cup sugar and continue to simmer. The more sugar you add, the sweeter are the mushrooms and the thicker the syrup. Simmer another 10 minutes, until the syrup just starts to become bubbly and frothy. Separate the candied mushrooms from the syrup by straining. Store the mushrooms and syrup in separate covered containers in the refrigerator.

Cook the sweet potato in water until tender. Drain, cool, and then place in a bowl and mash until smooth. Add the milk, butter, and eggs and stir to combine. In another bowl, combine the flour, salt, sugar, and yeast. Add the potato mixture to the flour mixture and stir until a shaggy dough forms. Empty the dough onto the counter and knead into a smooth ball. Return the dough to the bowl and cover. Let rise for about 1 hour.

While the dough is rising, mix the filling and cream cheese topping. Place all filling ingredients in a bowl and combine. Set aside. Next, combine all topping ingredients in a bowl and beat with an electric mixer until smooth.

FILLING

⅓ cup brown sugar

2 tbsp ground cinnamon

6 tbsp unsalted butter, room temperature

1 tsp vanilla

CREAM CHEESE TOPPING

8 oz cream cheese

2 cups icing sugar

2 tsp vanilla

1 tbsp lemon juice

Preheat the oven to 375°F. Line two cookie sheets with parchment and set aside. Tip the risen dough onto a clean, lightly floured surface. Cut the dough into two equal pieces. Roll one piece into a rectangle approximately 12 inches by 20 inches. Spread the filling on this rectangle. Roll the second ball of dough to the same size as the first. Place the second sheet of dough on top of the first. Gently roll with a rolling pin to seal these sheets together. With a sharp knife, cut the dough across the short end into 1-inch strips. You should have about 20 strips. Working one at a time, twist each dough strand, fold into a light knot, and tuck the ends under the bottom. Place on the prepared baking sheet. Cover the buns with a tea towel and let rise for about 30 minutes.

Bake for 25 to 30 minutes, until the tops are golden. Remove from the oven and add the cream cheese topping and candied chanterelles. Drizzle with a little syrup if desired. **MT**

RHUBARB CAKE

This recipe is from my husband's grandmother. It's a dark cake, and you may think you've overbaked it—but it is very moist and an excellent way to use up that bag of frozen rhubarb pieces at the bottom of the freezer.

2 cups all-purpose flour

1 tsp baking soda

1 tsp salt

½ cup shortening

1½ cups white sugar

1 egg

1 tsp vanilla

1 cup buttermilk or sour milk

1½ cups rhubarb, finely chopped

½ cup nuts

½ cup shredded coconut

½ cup brown sugar

½ tsp cinnamon

Preheat the oven to 350°F and grease a 9-inch square cake pan.

Cream the shortening and sugar until light and fluffy. Add the egg and vanilla and mix well. Sift together the flour, baking soda, and salt. Add the sifted dry ingredients to the creamed mixture alternately with milk. Fold in the rhubarb and nuts. Pour the batter into the prepared cake pan. Combine the coconut, brown sugar, and cinnamon, and sprinkle this mixture over the batter. Bake for 55 to 60 minutes or until a cake tester comes out clean. **MT**

Notes on Pickling

I always assumed that pickling was a long-held Newfoundland tradition until I started asking around. Much to my surprise, Nan Knight (my mother's mother) said that it wasn't something she, or her generation, did much. In my family at least, pickling really began in Mom's time.

When I was young, "pickling parties" seemed to go on for months. They started with spring bakeapples (cloudberries) and rhubarb pickles; then came gooseberry pickles and jam from the late-summer wild berries. Next came the fall garden pickling—zucchini pickles, bread and butter pickles, and, finally, cabbage pickles (last because cabbage could stay in the ground until frost).

We've included several pickle recipes in this book for you to enjoy. Try my mother-in-law Regina McCarthy's green tomato pickles, Mom's rhubarb pickles, and the many others we have collected from across the island.

The pickling and bottling process is different from that of meat bottling. Vegetables are first cooked in a vinegar and sugar recipe, preventing nasty bacterial growth. The hot pickled vegetables and liquid are poured into the bottles. Lids are screwed on and the bottles placed in a simmering water bath for 30 minutes. This is long enough to drive the air out of the bottles to seal them and preserve the colour and flavour of the vegetables.

RHUBARB PICKLES

These pickles are delicious served with any meat or vegetable dish.

8 cups fresh rhubarb, cut into ½-inch pieces

2 cups white vinegar

4 cups brown sugar

4 cups onion, diced

2 tsp ground cloves

4 tsp ground allspice

4 tsp ground cinnamon

2 tsp salt

Combine all ingredients in a large boiler. Bring to a boil and cook for 1 hour. Bottle while hot in clean, sterilized jars and lids. Refer to pickled fireweed (page 50) for the water bath process.

Lori McCarthy and her mother, Shirley Butler.

PICKLED FIREWEED with CORIANDER and CUMIN

These pickles are a great addition to a charcuterie board or a moose pastrami sandwich.

3 lb fireweed shoots, about 6 inches long

3 cups pickling vinegar

½ cup cider vinegar

1 cup water

¼ cup sea salt

½ cup sugar

2 tsp coriander seeds

2 tsp cumin seeds

2 tsp black peppercorns

4 garlic cloves, sliced

Bring a large pot of water to a boil and sterilize the jars. Bring a smaller pot of water to a simmer to heat the lids and soften the rubber seals.

Wash and trim the fireweed. Trim in half lengthwise to fit into the jars.

Combine the vinegar, salt, sugar, and water in a stainless-steel saucepan. Bring to a boil over medium heat, stirring until the salt and sugar dissolve. Reduce the heat and simmer until ready to fill the jars.

Divide the spices and garlic evenly between the sterilized jars, then pack tightly with the fireweed. Ladle the hot pickling liquid into the jars to cover the fireweed, leaving a ½-inch headspace. Wipe the mouths of the jars with a clean wet cloth. Lay the softened lids over the mouths of the jars and screw on the bands until just finger tight. Using a jar lifter, place the jars in the boiling water bath and process for 15 minutes.

Remove the jars from the water bath and let stand on a cooling rack, undisturbed, at room temperature until all the seals have popped. If a seal does not pop, you can reopen and process again or keep that jar in the refrigerator to use immediately. Store jars in a cool, dark place for up to a year. Refrigerate after opening. **MT**

Lacto-Fermentation

Lacto-fermentation, a simple fermentation process requiring only salt, water, vegetables, and time, is responsible for sauerkraut, kimchi, and other dishes. "Healthy" bacteria can survive a salty environment; those that might harm us do not. Even though this process is easy and accessible, I have yet to find an example of lacto-fermentation used traditionally in Newfoundland, though that's not to say it wasn't done—it's just another story I get to chase.

Brining was, however, common practice, especially with cabbage in the fall. Many have shared memories of barns and cellars with large buckets of cabbage in brine. From what I have gathered, the ratio of salt to water would have been too great to cultivate the lacto-fermentation bacteria. I regularly heard of the method of adding enough salt to the water to make a potato float. Then the cabbage could be submerged and weighed down to prevent mould from forming on the top.

In 2017, I first started experimenting with lacto-fermentation. There were failures—a lot of failures mostly in texture but in flavour too, ending in off-putting slimy concoctions that, frankly, weren't fit to eat. One of many successes has been with Japanese knotweed. These have happily lasted in my refrigerator for six to eight months once fermented.

FERMENTED JAPANESE KNOTWEED

Japanese knotweed, chopped in ½-inch pieces (peel the knotweed with a carrot peeler to remove the woody outer layer)

Water

Salt

Glass jar with a lid

Digital scale

Place the jar on the scale and tare it so that it reads zero. Fill the jar with peeled knotweed to 2 to 3 inches from the top. Add water until it is level with the top of the knotweed. Check and record the weight, which will be the knotweed and water combined.

Add 2 per cent of that weight in salt to your jar. Cover and shake or stir to dissolve the salt and place in a dark cupboard (at room temperature). Every day for seven to 10 days, carefully unscrew the lid to release the built-up gas. It many take three to four days or more before the gas gets going. I start tasting at day 5 to try and capture my preference in flavour and texture. Sometimes I stop the fermentation at day 5 and place the jar in the refrigerator; I have waited as long as 10 days with some vegetables. At day 10, place the jar in the refrigerator if you have not already done so, and enjoy with anything that needs a nice sour kick.

Harvesting Japanese knotweed
First off, you usually have only a week or so to harvest it before it's too tall to enjoy at its best.

In the early spring, just a few weeks after the snow has gone, head to where you know it grows. Pull away all of last year's tall, bamboolike stalks and you'll see the little pink shoots. The shoots are fantastic when picked at 1 to 2 inches and lightly sautéed in butter. Once they reach 4 to 8 inches and before the leaves unfurl, it's time to pick for lacto-fermentation.

Always pick responsibly and carefully, away from any contaminants. Knotweed usually grows within city limits in disturbed soils, which are not always suitable places for picking food. **LM**

SPRUCE TIP SYRUP

Freshly picked spring spruce tips

Brown sugar

Half fill a jar with spruce tips; add brown sugar to completely fill the jar. Cover and leave in the sun for a day or two, until the sugar starts to melt. Let cure in a cool, dark place until the contents turn liquid and no solid sugar remains. An occasional stir will help it along. When the sugar has completely dissolved (this could take 3 to 4 days), strain through a fine sieve and store in an airtight container. **MT**

Spruce tip sugar and spruce tip salt.

jiggs & reels

JULY
AUGUST
SEPTEMBER

"Come on you silver-sided warrior. Take it, take it, TAKE IT!"

–Rod Stowe, Mistaken Point, Upper Humber

> *"For the true angler, fishing produces a deep unspoken joy, born of longing for that which is quiet and peaceful and fostered by an inbred love of communing with nature."*

Thaddeus Norris, *The American Angler's Book* (1864)

The Salmon Angler's Journey

Salmon angling is a sport, a passion, an addiction, a frustration, and a host of other descriptive words (some of them four-lettered). Since this book is more than a collection of recipes—it is a personal journey for the authors—I decided to include these few words about my salmon angling personal journey.

I started salmon angling with my father when I was about 10 years old, some 60 years ago. My father is long gone but I never feel as close to him as I do when I am on the river. When I rise, play, or gently release a fish, I can still hear his instructions. Our local clergyman once asked my father why he did not attend Sunday service. His reply was that he never felt closer to God than on a fine Sunday morning at Flat Bay Brook, his favourite river. He always came home in a good mood after a day on the river, fish or no fish. I was not there to see him catch his first salmon, but I witnessed him land his last. He was just as excited at the end of his salmon angling journey as I am sure he was at the beginning. His advice was always to be hopeful and have respect for the water—a true sportsman.

I am not antisocial, but I like to fish alone. I don't like noise in the background when I am on the river. Salmon fishing used to clear my head after the work week, and even though I don't work anymore, it still clears my head. I am interested in all things in or around the river. The water—its colour, its depth, the light, the current, the wind on it, the insects on the surface—because all of these factors influence how you fish. I pay attention to the weather, because I am sure fish sense weather just as other animals, including humans, do. Many other things add to my enjoyment of being on the river, including birds in the bushes and on the water, beavers, moose, caribou, and other small animals that frequent the riverbank.

In my time as a salmon angler, I have seen changes in the number of salmon in the river. But the biggest change of all is the people. I do not see as many young people on the rivers, which is regrettable. Salmon angling is a wonderful family activity which teaches youth about nature, conservation, and family values. The lunchtime boil-up on the beach is as important as the fishing. I blame the computer age, in which speed and instant results are most important. Salmon angling has a steep learning curve, one which requires patience, disappointment, and a lot of time spent on the river to be successful.

I am coming to the end of my own salmon fishing journey. I don't walk to Mistaken Point on the Humber River anymore, but I can still fish Eva's Run on Flat Bay Brook and continue to be arthritically hopeful.

**By Bill Hudson
(father of Marsha Tulk)**

RECEIPE

Recipe for: Apricot raisin cake.
from the kitchen of: Roxy Hudson.

1½ cups dried apricot cut very
small.
1½ cups White Sugar.
2½ " flour. 4 eggs.
½ tsp. baking powder serves:
1 cup raisins.
½ " milk. 1 cup butter.
1 pkg. (8 oz) cream cheese.
1 tsp vanilla.

(Method). Cream butter, sugar,
cream cheese untie light x
smooth. Beat in eggs one
at a time. Add vanilla,
flour, bak. powder. Take enough
flour to flour fruit, fold in
last. Bake in cake pan (ones)

APRICOT RAISIN CAKE

In many communities in Newfoundland, it's a long-standing tradition to include a blank recipe card with a bridal shower invitation so that the bride-to-be has a collection of tried-and-true recipes to use during her married life. This recipe was given to me by my grandmother on my father's side. According to Roxy, "this makes a good cake for when company is around at summertime." She's right. This cake uses ingredients that most have in their pantries, just in case you have unexpected visitors during the summer.

1½ cups dried apricots, cut in small pieces

1 cup salted butter

1½ cups white sugar

8 oz cream cheese

2½ cups all-purpose flour

4 eggs

2 tsp baking powder

1 cup raisins

½ cup milk

1 tsp vanilla

Preheat oven to 300°F. Sprinkle a little flour over the apricots, shake or stir to coat, and set aside. In a large mixing bowl, cream the butter, sugar, and cream cheese together until light and smooth. Beat in the eggs one at a time. Add the vanilla, flour, and baking powder. Fold in the fruit. Bake in a well-greased tube pan for 1½ hours.

This cake freezes well. Cut it in quarters, wrap first with plastic wrap and then aluminum foil, and freeze for up to six months. **MT**

Wild Caraway

I always enjoy when a subject as simple as a caraway seed evokes a wealth of personal anecdotes and family histories.

My father asked about Lori's Wild Caraway Rye Bread. I told him how Lori's mom, as a child, picked caraway in a few small patches on the east coast of Newfoundland. My father immediately recalled his mother collecting the caraway seeds in Heatherton, on the island's west coast. He also had an explanation for how this apparently hard-to-find seed came to Newfoundland.

Caraway is usually a cultivated plant, similar in appearance to other members of the carrot family, with finely divided, feathery leaves, growing to a height of about 24 inches. The main flower stem has small white or pink flowers. The caraway fruit, commonly called seeds, are crescent-shaped, about 2 millimetres long, with five pale ridges. The fruit has an anise-like flavour and aroma that come from its essential oils. Usually used whole in recipes, you get little bursts of caraway as you munch on them. In some places, caraway is considered a noxious invasive weed and is eradicated so that it won't invade crop-specific fields.

Caraway is a prolific seeder and escapes cultivated gardens easily. It has been used as far back as Roman times and appears in Austrian, German, Norwegian, Eastern European, Middle Eastern, and many other cuisines. But Newfoundland's plants likely came from Scottish immigrants who commonly used caraway in their traditional cooking and baking, including in a digestive cookie called an Abernathy biscuit. The caraway plants found on Newfoundland's east coast likely originated with more affluent Scots, while those on the west coast arrived in the Codroy Valley via Scottish farmers from Nova Scotia and Cape Breton. Some of these farmers moved along the coast, looking for good farmland, and settled in the Robinsons and Heatherton areas.

My father doesn't recall anyone growing caraway in a kitchen garden in Heatherton, because you could get all you wanted in late summer along the borders of hayfields. After the hay was cut and harvested, the plants would be in fruit and easy to forage; the hay-cutting machinery could only go so close to the fences, leaving the caraway exposed to easily pick. He doesn't know how his grandmother MacDonald used caraway in her cooking, only that she would collect it for her pantry.

We have included caraway seeds in many of our recipes such as the Wild Caraway Rye Bread and Pickled Carrots. **MT**

WILD CARAWAY RYE BREAD

I have listened to Mom tell me the story many times of when she was a child and being sent up in Nannie's garden to pick wild caraway. She would bring it home and Nan (her mother) would dry the caraway. It took me 20 years to find this wild caraway and it holds a precious place in my heart now. I harvest it every year.

1 tsp active dry yeast

½ cup warm water

1 tsp sugar

2 cups rye flour (stone ground or light rye both work but will create different textures)

¾ cup blackstrap or fancy molasses

⅓ cup shortening

2 cups boiling water

2 tsp salt

½ cup wild yeast starter

1 tbsp wild caraway seeds + more for sprinkling on top (or substitute purchased caraway)

6 to 7 cups all-purpose flour

1 egg (for egg wash)

To bloom the yeast, add it to ½ cup warm water and 1 teaspoon sugar and set it aside for 15 minutes. This ensures that the yeast is still beautifully active.

In another bowl, combine the rye flour, blackstrap molasses, shortening, boiling water, salt, wild yeast starter, and caraway. Let cool to room temperature, giving it a stir every few minutes to cool it off faster. When cooled, gradually knead in 6 to 7 cups all-purpose flour, until the dough has come together and is no longer sticky. Cover and let rest for 10 minutes, then knead again until you have created a smooth, elastic dough. Let rise until double in size.

Punch down, cut into three pieces. Preheat the oven to 375°F. Roll the dough into balls and set aside on parchment or a greased pan to rise for 1 hour or until double in size. Brush the loaves with a beaten egg and sprinkle some caraway seeds on top. Make a few cuts along the top to allow the bread to expand. Bake for 40 minutes. **LM**

Smoking a moose heart.

FIRESIDE SMOKED MOOSE HEART TARTARE & GRILLED MARROW

To enjoy this very special food moment, start with your drink of choice and gather your favourite people to sit around the fire with.

Smoking the heart is optional but worth it. The day we smoked the heart we skewered the heart with an alder stick and smoked it with alder leaves and branches over the fire for about 30 minutes. You can use any cold smoke method (see page 21) you are familiar with.

As you enjoy the tartare, start cooking the marrow. By the time the tartare has been devoured, the bones will be ready to be moved onto your board to enjoy.

MOOSE HEART TARTARE

1 cup moose heart, smoked if desired

¼ cup finely diced shallots or green onion

¼ cup finely diced beach lovage or parsley

1 egg yolk

¼ tbsp capers

1 tbsp Newfoundland Salt Company's alder salt or salt of choice

This is not a recipe so much as an assembly.

First, get a wooden cutting board or dinner plate to serve the tartare on. Each person should pile tartare on their own slices of bread, dressing them as they wish.

Hand-mince or dice the moose heart, avoiding the fat and any veins. Pile it in a mound at the centre of the board or plate. Make separate little piles of shallots, lovage, salt, and pickled capers around the meat. Place the egg yolk in the half-shell or in a little dish and set it in the middle of the meat.

Grill the bread or, even better, get everyone to grill their own as you sit around the fire. With grilled bread in hand, start with a light spread of sauce, pile on a little meat and each of the toppings to taste. Add some egg yolk and finish with a sprinkle of salt.

SAUCE

2 tbsp mayonnaise

2 tbsp plain yogurt

1 tsp ground juniper berries

Pinch of salt

Pinch of pepper

Squeeze of lemon juice

MOOSE MARROW

2 pieces of moose chin bone, sawed lengthways by your favourite butcher

Crusty bread, sliced and ready to be grilled

The marrow will take between 12 and 15 minutes to cook, depending on the heat in the coals. We had a medium heat going on the fire when we did this; you can also use a barbecue or broil in the oven. Sprinkle salt and pepper on the marrow. Start by cooking with the cut-side down for 3 to 5 minutes, just enough to give it a good sear. Turn the bone over and finish cooking marrow side up. You'll need enough time for the heat to cook the marrow from the bottom up; 10 to 12 minutes should do. It is important not to leave it on the heat too long; you don't want the precious marrow to fall out on the fire. You'll know it's done when the marrow pulls away slightly from the sides of the bone. With a little scoop, the marrow will easily release from the bone. **LM**

Cabbage Sauerkraut and
Moose Pastrami Sandwich.

CABBAGE SAUERKRAUT WITH WILD CARAWAY

This was one of my first fermenting recipes. It is so easy and the perfect complement to moose pastrami for sandwiches. If you make it, you will never buy it from a store again. If you don't have wild caraway seeds, you may substitute store-bought.

**2 lb cabbage,
about 1 medium head**

4 tsp sea salt

1 tbsp wild caraway seeds

Remove any damaged exterior leaves from the cabbage. Cut the cabbage in quarters through the core. Remove the core, then slice the cabbage quarters into strips no wider than 1/8 inch thick.

Toss the cabbage and salt in a large bowl and let it rest for about 20 minutes to soften and release its juice. Squeeze the cabbage by hand to soften it even further and release more juice.

After about 30 minutes, when the cabbage has become limp and released much of its juice, transfer it to a large Mason jar. Pack the cabbage tightly into the jar using a wooden spoon so that it continues to release its liquid and the air bubbles are squeezed out. Continue packing the cabbage into the jar until the jar is almost full and the cabbage completely submerged. Place a large piece of cabbage leaf over the top and weight it down so that the cabbage rests just below the surface of the juice. A small sterilized beach rock works well for a weight. Loosely place the jar lid on the jar.

Let the cabbage ferment at room temperature, away from direct sunlight, for about 1 month or until it to your taste. Remove the weight, tighten the lid, and refrigerate. It will keep from 6 months to a year. **MT**

MOOSE PASTRAMI

This pastrami makes a delicious sandwich with sauerkraut on Wild Caraway Rye Bread (page 69).

THE (MOSTLY) WILD SPICE MIX:

1 tbsp crushed dried sweet gale

1 tbsp dried alder catkins

1 tbsp sweet gale buds crushed

1 tbsp peppercorns

1 tsp crushed red chili

Use a boneless piece of meat—I like to use the brisket, the flank, or an inside/outside round cut.

To make pastrami, use the Corned Moose recipe on page 117 and add the spice mix to the brine. **LM**

The Picnic

Wicker baskets, backpacks, coolers, wooden crates, pails, buckets, or crumpled brown paper bags full of everything and anything edible—what is it about a picnic or a boil-up in Newfoundland that is so special? The mere mention of having one draws people together to prepare, pack, and plod out into a favourite patch of woods or clamber into a boat to find that perfect stretch of beach.

As I looked through my grandfather's photographs, I was surprised by how many eating occasions were documented. Groups of people both young and old gathered around a decorative lacy cotton cloth on the ground. Scattered among the baskets and pails are china teacups and mugs filled with copper kettle tea or instant coffee, cans of fruit salad, and tins of baked goods waiting to be smeared with homemade preserves. It seems they just took whatever was in the pantry, left over in the icebox, or could be cooked up over the fire.

Some of my best picnics are my husband and I walking the dog at 7 a.m. just 10 minutes down the road to overlook the beach with a bottle of water, a coffee press, and a few eggs to boil.

I asked my younger son if he had any idea why we would pack up as a family and take off to some trail or park or pond for the day with just a bag of food and a few pots on our backs. His response was, "I don't really know. It must be in our DNA." He also remarked that he doesn't remember us *not* doing just that. Even my boy's stroller had skis for the winter. If we couldn't go away for a few days or a week-long excursion, we would always make time for at least an afternoon of enjoying some fresh air and a mug-up.

While I was scanning and editing these old photographs of picnics, I noticed the similarities between all the scenes. At least three generations were in each photograph, and the kids were not off on their own but intermingled with the adults. To be a fly on a chunk of picnic cheese eavesdropping on the conversations in those groups! The uncomplicated and plentiful food meant that they could concentrate on the important things. Maybe there's no need to ask why we love a good picnic. Maybe we get out there for no other reason than to get outside for a few hours, together. **MT**

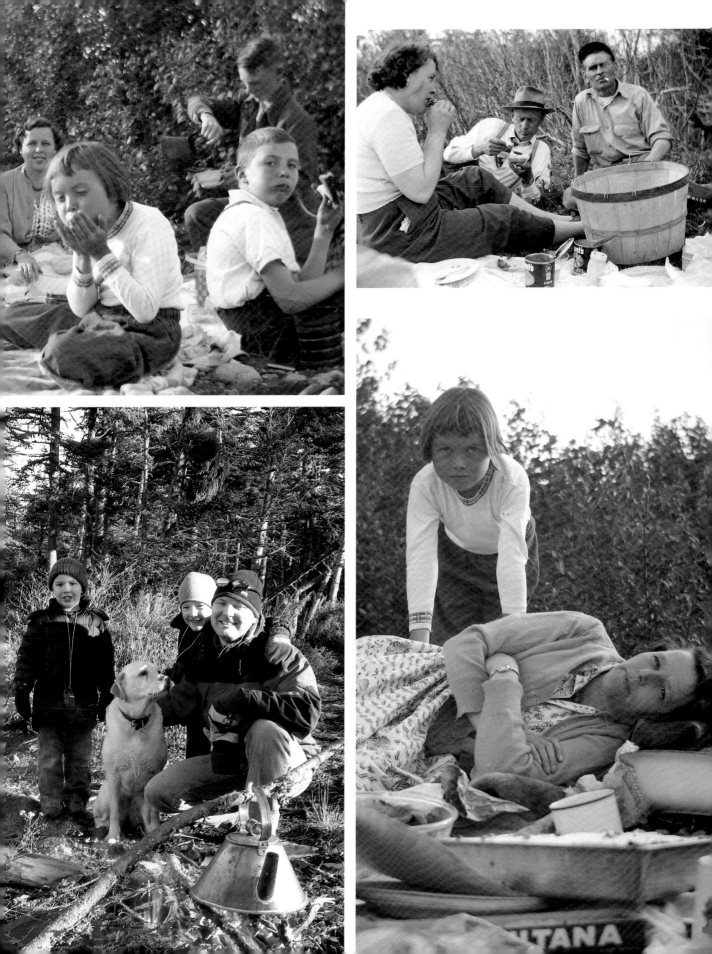

HALIBUT TACOS

Feel free to substitute flat-leaf parsley or cilantro for lovage in this recipe, according to your taste and availability.

1 lb skinless halibut fillets, cut into 1-inch chunks

MARINADE

3 limes

2 cloves garlic, quartered

1 cup lovage, leaves and tender stems (cilantro is a good substitute)

1 bunch green onions, white and green sections, chopped, divided

2 tsp ground cumin

1 tsp sea salt

3 tsp extra-virgin olive oil

To make the marinade, finely grate the zest of 1 lime and place in a food processor. Squeeze in the juice of that lime plus the juice of 2 more limes. Add the garlic, lovage, half of the green onions, cumin, and 1 teaspoon salt. Pulse until roughly chopped. Add 3 teaspoons olive oil and 2 tablespoons water. Blend until the mixture becomes smooth.

To make the slaw, toss the shredded cabbage, 2 tablespoons marinade, the rest of the green onions, the juice of 1 lime, 2 tablespoons olive oil, and ½ teaspoon salt in a large bowl. Set aside.

SLAW

3 cups shredded cabbage

½ tsp sea salt

1 lime

2 tbsp extra-virgin olive oil

CREMA

1 lime

⅔ cup sour cream

6 to 8 corn tortillas

Toss the chunks of halibut in a bowl with the remainder of the marinade. Marinate for about 30 minutes.

Combine the juice of the remaining lime with the sour cream in a small serving bowl.

To cook the halibut, skewer the chunks on barbeque sticks of your choice. (We like to use short alder branches with the leaves still on the ends, but regular store-bought skewers will work fine.) Heat the grill to a medium-high heat and oil it to prevent the halibut from sticking. Grill the halibut for about 6 minutes, turning to grill on all sides. Place on a plate and cover to keep warm.

To assemble the tacos, quickly grill the tortillas on the barbeque at the same medium-high heat just long enough to colour and heat through. Watch closely— they burn quickly. Divide the fish between the shells and top with the slaw, sour cream mixture, and salsa or hot sauce of choice. **MT**

LIME AND CARAWAY SALMON GRAVLAX

Salmon (or trout) fillet, fresh, skin on and pin bones removed

White sugar

Sea salt

Limes, zested and thinly sliced

Fresh caraway or dill fronds

Gently rinse the fillet and pat dry. Cut off the thin belly section; it cures much quicker than the rest. If you have one large fillet, halve it.

Prepare the appropriate amount of salt/sugar mix for the weight of the salmon. Zest 1 lime and slice the needed number of lime slices.

Place a layer of plastic wrap on top of a dish large enough to accommodate the length of the fillet. Lay the two pieces of fillet, skin side down, on the plastic wrap next to each other. Shake the salt/sugar mix over the thickest parts of the fillet, more on the thick and less on the thin ends. Do not go to the edges, but keep it in the middle.

Roughly chop the caraway fronds and spread half on 1 fillet; keep the lime from direct contact with the flesh of the salmon (the flesh cooks due to the lime's acidity). Sprinkle the zest over the caraway. Place the lime slices on top of the zest and cover with the remaining caraway. Quickly flip the remaining fillet on top of the other, salt/sugar side down and skin side up. Wrap the fillets tightly with the plastic wrap that was placed under them. Wrap tightly several more times, with at least one layer wrapped lengthwise. Put the wrapped fillets in the dish and refrigerate. The dish is important: liquid will be released from the salmon while it cures, no matter how tightly it is wrapped. (If it is wrapped tightly enough, a weight is not needed on top, as many gravlax recipes call for.)

Over the next two days, flip the salmon once in the morning and once in the evening. After two days, it should be cured. Unwrap, remove the caraway and limes, thinly slice, and enjoy. **MT**

Follow the chart for proper proportions for the salmon, rounding up if between measurements.

Weight of salmon	Salt	Sugar	Limes
3.4 lb	2 tbsp	6 tbsp	6 slices
2.8 lb	5 tsp	5 tbsp	5 slices
2.3 lb	4 tsp	4 tbsp	4 slices
1.7 lb	3 tsp	3 tbsp	3 slices
1.1 lb	2 tsp	2 tbsp	2 slices
0.6 lb	1 tsp	1 tbsp	1 slice

TAILGATE LIMPETS AND PERIWINKLES

Limpets and periwinkles (also called winkles or whelk) are aquatic snails; limpets have a conical shell, while periwinkles have the familiar spiral snail shell. On the west coast of Newfoundland, they are sometimes referred to as *concalou*. I love this name! Picking limpets and periwinkles was not part of my childhood but it is of my children's. It has become part of our family tradition: a new practice born out of pure joy—less about necessity, as food traditions were in Nan's time. These traditions will continue to grow, change, and develop, as they always have. This development of culture matters to me and motivates me to continue.

The first time I made this was during my first year with an official guide licence. I had taken several guys from Maine salmon fishing on the Salmonier river. As inexperienced as I was, I needed some help, and I enlisted a local guide and friend to accompany us. Our first stop of the day was a favourite ocean tidal pool of mine, and I was determined to show our guests that a few creatures picked along the way would prove to be a tasty treat. To pick these little aquatic treasures, at low tide roll up your pants and wade out a few feet. Our timing was perfect and we managed to pick a couple of cups of them before we headed off for our day's plans. Just before we reached the river, I hauled down the tailgate, opened up the butane burner, and fried them all up with butter, garlic, and shallots. I believe the guys were surprised that the snails were so good and by the spontaneity of a meal picked along the way.

Limpets and periwinkles do not need to be purged of sand as mussels do. As they live attached to rocks, they are algae eaters, and do not contain any gritty sand that might get caught in your teeth. They are easily harvested at low tide and, with no legal limit, you can take enough to fill your puddick (stomach).

To prepare them, simply melt 2 to 3 tablespoons butter, and add 1 clove minced fresh garlic and 1 small minced shallot. Fry just till golden, toss in a couple of handfuls (about 2 cups) of mollusks, shells and all, and a glug (about 1/4 cup) of beer. I'm partial to Quidi Vidi Iceberg beer, but you can use your favourite. Boil for 2 minutes, turn off the heat, and pick away! I like to finish these with chopped beach lovage for a nice licorice taste. Limpets fall out of their shells, but periwinkles need a safety pin to do the trick. **LM**

PRESERVED CHANTERELLES IN OIL

I usually preserve my precious chanterelle harvest by cleaning them and sorting by size (thanks, Mom). I sauté the small and medium ones in unsalted butter and then pack them in muffin tins to freeze, so that each frozen brick is about ½ cup.

Funghi sott'olio is a wonderful way to preserve this mushroom in oil with a bit of spice. This is by far the nicest chanterelle recipe I have tried. The mushrooms can be dressed up on a charcuterie board or dressed down on the trail with cheese, moose jerky, and a piece of crusty bread. My kids called that a fancy trail lunch. This recipe is great for smaller mushrooms. Save the larger ones to cook fresh and enjoy immediately. Use your favourite good-quality olive oil in this recipe.

4 lb chanterelles, thoroughly cleaned and trimmed

2 cups water

2 cups white wine vinegar, plus extra if needed

Sea salt, to taste

4 hot chilies, whole and dried

2 tbsp fresh oregano leaves

2 tbsp fresh sweet gale leaves

1 cup olive oil

In a large saucepan, bring water to a boil and add vinegar. Place the cleaned mushrooms in the liquid. Gently boil for about 7 minutes. Add more vinegar if needed to cover the mushrooms. Keep the mushrooms submerged while boiling.

Drain the mushrooms with a slotted spoon and lay them on paper towel or a clean dish towel and gently press out the excess vinegar with another clean towel. Lay the mushrooms on another clean, dry towel and let them air-dry until they are no longer wet but still soft. This may take 30 minutes to several hours. Once the mushrooms are dry but still pliable, place them in a bowl with the oregano leaves, sweet gale leaves, and salt. Toss to coat thoroughly.

Pack the mixture in cleaned and sterilized Mason jars. Place 1 dried chili in each jar. Add 2 spoonfuls of mushroom mixture at a time, then pour in just enough olive oil to cover them. Add more mushroom and oil layers until the jar is full and the mushrooms are completely submerged. Remove as much air between the mushrooms as possible. Making sure that the mushrooms are completely submerged in oil, screw on the lids and place the jars in the refrigerator for at least one week so that the flavours of the chilies, sweet gale, and oregano are absorbed. If kept submerged in oil and refrigerated, these mushrooms can last for up to 6 months. **MT**

PICKLED CARROTS WITH CORIANDER, CARAWAY, AND NETTLE SEEDS

For years I have had a few small raised-bed vegetable gardens. Nothing too ambitious, just a small selection of the more popular plants and herbs for personal use. I first planted a garden when my husband and I bought our first house. My kids grew up running around the backyard in summer and, when they got hungry, they picked peas off the vine or plucked a carrot out of the ground and washed it under water from the hose. Even our Labrador retrievers got into the act if plants hung over the edge of the planter. To this day, I plant a garden and my two teenage boys still snack on fresh vegetables when they pass by the planter.

But my nemesis is the carrot. I love fresh carrots straight out of the ground. But I cannot seem to grow them to any size. This isn't that much of a surprise—most years I don't even water the garden regularly because we are away on summer road trips camping, canoeing, and fishing, trying to make the most of our short summers. So I usually end up with hundreds of very small but tasty carrots. This recipe was designed to put them to good use. My carrots pack perfectly into Mason jars and these pickles are a wonderful addition to a charcuterie board.

---

3 lb small carrots

3 cups white vinegar

½ cup cider vinegar

¼ cup sea salt

¼ cup white sugar

1 cup water

2 tsp coriander seeds

2 tsp wild caraway seeds

2 tsp nettle seeds, optional

4 cloves garlic, peeled

Clean and sterilize Mason jars. Bring a large pot of water to a boil to be ready to process the filled jars. Bring a smaller pot of water to a simmer to soften new Mason jar lids.

Scrub the carrots with a vegetable brush and remove the tops and any imperfections. If some carrots are longer than 4 inches or fatter than the others, trim to the same size as the majority.

Combine the vinegars, salt, sugar, and water in a medium saucepan. Bring to a boil over medium heat, stirring until the salt and sugar have dissolved. Reduce to a simmer to keep the pickling liquid hot until the jars have been filled.

If you don't have wild caraway seeds, substitute with store-bought.

Divide the dried spices and garlic evenly between the sterilized jars, then pack tightly with carrots. Ladle the hot pickling liquid into the jars to cover all the carrots, leaving a ½-inch headspace. Wipe the jar tops clean for a good seal. Place the heated, softened lids on top of each jar and add the bands, tightening them to just finger tight. Place the filled jars in the water bath and process for 15 minutes.

Remove the jars from the water bath and let stand, undisturbed, until the tops pop, indicating a good seal. The seal is good if the lid is depressed and will stay on the jar tightly without the band. If a jar has not sealed, reprocess it or refrigerate it for immediate use. Store jars in a cool, dark place for up to a year. Refrigerate after opening. **MT**

Makes 6 x 500 mL Mason jars.

CRABAPPLE BACON JAM

In my neighbourhood, there are a number of productive apple trees on homesteads and in long-abandoned farm fields. If the tree is on private property, I always knock and ask the owner if I can pick a few apples; and if the homeowner wants some, I pick for them while I'm there. Sometimes I even go back with whatever dish I made from their apples and give them half. Many of these old trees were planted by the original owners of the property many years ago.

My grandparents had a large apple orchard behind their house. As kids, my brother and I spent hours climbing and eating apples from the trees. My grandfather had long wooden poles with V-notched pieces of scrap metal attached to the end with recycled nails. It was great fun to raise these poles to the sky and try to pick the biggest apples off the highest branches. Every year I go back and pick a few basketfuls and am amazed by the number of apples that go unused. If you have a lonely apple tree in your neighbourhood with its limbs sagging and begging to be picked, go knock on the owner's door. You will more than likely acquire some delicious fresh apples plus have an interesting chat with a newfound friend.

1½ lb thick-cut homemade bacon

2 cups onion, finely chopped

1 tbsp garlic, minced

2 cups crabapples, cores removed and roughly chopped

½ tsp ground ginger

¼ tsp cayenne pepper

1 tbsp Dijon mustard

½ cup spiced rum

1/3 cup malt vinegar

1 cup spruce tip syrup (page 54)

Sauté the bacon pieces in a large skillet over medium heat until crisp. Drain the rendered fat from the bacon with a slotted spoon and place the pieces on paper towels. Reserve 1 tablespoon of the bacon grease in the pan; discard the rest.

Add the onions to the same pan and cook until soft. Add the garlic and apples and sauté for another 4 to 5 minutes. Add the rest of the ingredients, including the bacon pieces. Stir to combine and bring to a boil. Reduce to a simmer. Stir occasionally until most of the liquid has evaporated but the mixture is still jamlike and syrupy. Either keep the jam chunky or puree in a food processor to make it more spreadable.

Transfer the jam to clean Mason jars. Serve immediately or refrigerate for up to a month. **MT**

Date: Feb 5/2021
ents: Crabapple
Bacon Jam

CHANTERELLE AND ONION JAM

4 onions, peeled,
halved and thinly sliced

2 cups fresh chanterelles,
quartered

2 tbsp olive oil

2 garlic cloves, minced

1 tbsp fresh oregano

½ cup Newman's port

1 cup vegetable stock

1 tsp salt

1 tbsp sugar

Heat the olive oil in a large frying pan over moderate heat. Add the onions, chanterelles, garlic, and oregano. Fry 5 to 8 minutes until the onions are softened. Add the port and let it sizzle for a few moments before adding the stock, salt, and sugar. Bring to a simmer and reduce the heat to low.

Cook for 1 hour uncovered, stirring regularly. Add water if required to maintain a creamy consistency.

After 1 hour, turn up the heat and cook off any remaining liquid. Remove from the heat and cool completely. Store in a Mason jar in the refrigerator. **MT**

GOOSEBERRY PICKLES

This is Mom's recipe. It's a family favourite and bottles of pickles are often shared, especially for Christmas. It seems that gooseberries have become scarcer; picking them is on Mom's mind often through the late summer. "I'll have to check the gooseberries now soon," I often hear her say. Some days I think she must have the bushes hidden in the woods somewhere.

Gooseberries and black currants were brought here from England and Ireland back in the day and planted around homesteads for jam and other preserves. Sometimes you'll find bushes in a field in a community without any trace of a house. It's a reminder of a bygone generation—with bounty left for the next.

These pickles have a jamlike consistency and are usually served with a cold plate, a bit of leftover meat roast, or on the side of any rich meal.

8 cups gooseberries, cleaned

4 cups onion, chopped

4 cups white or brown sugar

2¼ cups white vinegar

2 tsp cloves, powdered

4 tsp allspice

4 tsp cinnamon

2 tsp salt

Combine all ingredients, bring to a boil, and simmer for 1½ hours, stirring occasionally to prevent sticking. Pour into hot sterilized Mason jars.

Process in a water bath (see page 50 for detailed safe bottling procedure). **LM**

Makes 6 x 500 ml Mason jars.

ROXY'S ZUCCHINI PICKLES

M y grandmother Roxy says that mustard powder or bottled mustard can be used to replace the mustard seeds in a pinch. Process the bottles for 15 minutes—a little longer (if you have to hang your clothes on the line while the pickles are boiling) is okay. When you hear the jars "crack, crack," you know they are sealing. **MT**

12 cups fresh zucchini, cubed

4 large onions, cubed

2 red peppers, cubed

2 green peppers, cubed

⅓ cup pickling salt

3 cups white vinegar

4 cups white sugar

3 tbsp cornstarch

2 tsp celery seed

2 tsp mustard seed

2 tsp turmeric

Combine the chopped vegetables with salt, cover with cold water, and soak 12 hours. Drain and rinse. Place all vegetables in a large pot. Add the remaining ingredients. Bring to a boil and cook for 15 minutes. Spoon into hot sterilized jars and seal.

Recipe by Roxy Hudson

ROSE PETAL SUGAR

2 cups fresh rose petals

1 cup white sugar

To dry the petals, use a dehydrator set on 140°F for approximately 4 hours, or use your oven. For the oven method, lay the petals on a wire rack on top of a cookie sheet, spreading them out as much as possible so that they are not overlapping. Place the cookie sheet in the oven at its lowest setting. Place a wooden spoon in the oven door to keep it ajar so that the moisture can escape. Check the petals every 20 minutes until they have dried.

Use either a food processor or mortar and pestle to finely crush 1 cup of the dried petals. Add this to 1 cup sugar and mix thoroughly. Store in a dry airtight container for up to a year. **MT**

The Outfitter Tent

One of my children's first camping experiences was in an outfitter tent. As my husband and I are avid outdoors people, we wanted to expose our two boys to camping at a young age and give them an appreciation of being outside in nature.

We did not buy a 30-foot travel trailer as many of our friends did. Instead, I bought a 12 by 12-foot outfitter tent with a wood stove, cots, sleeping bags, and a little table with benches. Our go-to spot to camp was in Loop L in Terra Nova National Park. A very popular spot for families with younger kids, it had a playground in the middle of the loop, plus a comfort station with toilets and showers. The playground was very convenient—parents did not have to chase their wandering kids all over the park; they could stay in their own campsite or visit the cookhouse and let the kids converge on the slides and swings and wander around the loop comfortably.

We usually booked Canada Day to go to the park, and on this particular weekend we arrived in a downpour. Our campsite was right next to the cookhouse shelter and it was being used by all of the families camped in the loop, cooking up a feed and hiding from the rain. We left the kids and dogs in the truck and started setting up our site for the long weekend. As my husband and I set out the parts to the tent, I could hear the occupants of the cookhouse commenting on what a sin it was that we had to set up in such weather. They asked us if they could help, especially when they found out that we had two small kids in our truck. We thanked them, but politely declined, since we had become quite adept at putting up the tent in record time. The number of watching eyes from the crowd next door increased. The tent grew bigger and higher. By the time the chimney from the wood stove started to smoke, curiosity got the better of them. For the rest of the weekend, we gave tours of "Tent-zilla" (what the kids named it) and had a wonderful Canada Day.

I've always wondered if any of the sites we camped in was the one in which my grandparents set up their outfitter tent when they travelled across the island as far as the highway would take them. At that time, the highway was just being constructed and Terra Nova National Park was in its infancy. It took from 1962 to 1971 for the highway from Port aux Basques to St. John's to be completed. It must have been quite an adventure to be one of the first people to travel across the island by road instead of by train.

There's nothing better than the sounds outside the tent walls putting you to sleep, the bone-warming heat from the wood stove, and the smell of freshly perked coffee bubbling away on the stovetop in the morning. A great way to slow down, disconnect from the modern world, and reconnect to only what is immediately around you. Lloyd Colbourne, in his *Newfoundland Outdoors—The Story*, had it right: "Our camping gear: tent, camp stove and sleeping bags was our hotel away from home and just as cozy." **MT**

Matt Butler (Lori's grandfather)
fishing for trout.

on the hunt

OCTOBER
NOVEMBER
DECEMBER

"West coast rabbits are almost always fatter than those on this end of her."

–Matt Butler,
Bauline North

The Paunch

I'll never forget the rush on an early October morning, 2019—opening archery day—when I got the call that the b'ys (hunters carrying the Rotary charity licence) had the moose down. I went into a scramble to get on site for the paunching. My first moose paunch.

That day I realized how lucky I had been the year before when I did not manage to shoot a moose, up in the woods by myself. Paunching the moose is a big job. But this day was amazing, landing us over 400 pounds of meat. In the weeks that followed, many of our Rotarians came together to make the brine, clean the meat, and get it into cure for a salt moose fundraiser.

In 2017 the Rotary of St. John's East reached out to me for help with their charity moose. Here in Newfoundland and Labrador, charity licences are available to registered charities that wish to apply; the meat is used for community fundraisers and given to churches to be used in meal programs. This was a great opportunity for a give-back project for the community. That year, along with some help from the other Rotarians and the team at Merchant Tavern, spearheaded by my cousin Alex, we turned 200 pounds of moose into salt meat. It was vacuum packed and sold to raise money for several local organizations.

The Rotary has become a focus for my community work. It's been a rewarding journey. So many projects happen annually inside Rotary, but my pride sits with the annual moose hunt. *LM*

CORNED MOOSE MEAT

5 lb (2.25 kg) moose meat

1 lb 5 oz (600 g) salt, non-iodized

1 tbsp black peppercorns

2 bay leaves

6 juniper berries

1 oz (30 g) Prague powder No. 1/Cure #1

1 gallon + 4 cups (5 litres) water

1 onion, in quarters

Bring to a boil 4 cups water, salt, pepper, bay leaves, juniper berries, and Prague powder. Make sure the salt and Prague powder dissolve. Let cool completely before pouring into a large nonreactive container. Add an additional gallon of cold water. Once the liquid is fully chilled, add the pieces of moose and weight it down with a plate to completely submerge the meat in the liquid. Place the filled container in the refrigerator or outside in a shed, if it is cold enough, for 10 days. Give the meat a stir several times throughout the curing time to redistribute the cure around all pieces of the meat.

After 10 days, the meat is ready. It can stay in the curing liquid in a cool area for up to 3 months. During this time, you can remove pieces of the meat as you need it. To store the meat for a longer term, pour off the brine, rinse the meat, and put meal-sized portions in vacuum or zipper type bags and freeze.

When you are ready to cook the moose, give each piece a good rinse. You do not need to soak this meat like traditional salt meat—it's a very light salt brine, so you do not even need to change the water when cooking. Place the meat in clean fresh water, enough to cover the meat by about 3 inches, and bring to a boil. Turn down and simmer for 2 to 3 hours until tender. You may need to add additional water while simmering. **LM**

MOOSE CARPACCIO WITH SWEET GALE AIOLI

This dish is usually made as soon as the moose shows up home or, better yet, in the woods. It's another dish Dad won't go handy to; he says, "it's still callin'." Most of you reading would understand this but, just to clarify, he means that it's so raw the moose may as well be still in the woods calling out.

1 piece moose tenderloin (2–3 inches thick, 6–8 inches long)

Salt and pepper

4 tbsp butter

2 tsp canola oil

1 egg yolk

1 tsp sweet gale (rosemary can be substituted)

2 tsp white vinegar

½ tsp Dijon mustard

¼ cup sunflower oil

½ clove garlic

Grilled crusty bread to serve

To prepare the meat, season well with salt and pepper on all sides. Heat a heavy bottomed frying pan to medium-high heat. Add the butter and oil. Add the meat right away. Give the moose a quick sear, rolling it around to sear all edges. This should only take 2 to 3 minutes in total. Place the moose on a plate and put it in the freezer for about 1 hour to stiffen up so that it can be thinly sliced.

While the meat is chilling, prepare the aioli. Place the egg yolk, sweet gale, vinegar, garlic, mustard, and a pinch of salt and pepper in a countertop blender (or use a container and a hand blender). Slowly add the oil in a steady stream while the blender is running. Stop the blender when you have the desired consistency. You should end up with a runny, creamy, dressing-like consistency (not as thick as mayonnaise). As a side note, leftover aioli makes an excellent salad dressing.

To plate, remove the meat from the freezer and slice thinly. Lay the meat flat on a plate and drizzle with the aioli and a little olive oil. Finish with a sprinkle of salt and freshly ground pepper. I love to add a few bitter berries, such as black or red currants, thinly sliced. I add whole leaves of sheep and wood sorrel, but sliced radicchio or fresh lemon balm can be used as well. Top with any edible flowers you have available, plus a few pickled mushrooms. **LM**

A Beautiful Discovery

This was a beautiful discovery for me. Having ever only eaten beef bresaola, and only away, in big cities, I was determined to take moose to new heights back home. My first thought was that there is no good reason not to swap out the cuts of beef for moose. I have been making moose bresaola since 2015—I put one up in October and it was ready for Christmas. It makes a great conversation piece when friends and family come over.

The beauty with making bresaola is that you can buy beef to experiment on a few times before you take out that precious moose and make something that you may not love—though I haven't found anyone yet who doesn't love it. Well, maybe Dad. He won't touch the stuff.

You'll need to wait until the fall, when the threat of flies has completely gone and the nights are down to 5° to 6°C and the days less than 10°C. Some years it's the end of October before I can start curing meat because of the warm temperatures and because I hang it in the old drafty shed out back.

MOOSE BRESAOLA

3 lb moose (or beef) eye of round roast, no more than 3 inches in diameter

0.9 oz (25 g) kosher salt

1 oz (30 g) sugar

0.14 oz (4 g) Prague Powder #2 (or Cure #2 / DC curing salt #2)

0.14 oz (4 g) black pepper, freshly ground

0.8 oz (7 g) fresh sweet gale or rosemary, chopped

8 juniper berries, crushed with the side of a knife

Trim all visible fat, sinew, and silver skin from the moose meat. Place the remaining ingredients in a spice or coffee grinder and grind into a fine powder. Weigh the meat and record it (this is the "green weight"). Rub half of the spice cure all over the meat, rubbing it in well. Place the reserved cure in a small, covered container for later use. Place the prepared meat in a resealable storage bag and refrigerate for 7 days, turning it every couple of days to redistribute the cure.

Remove the meat from the bag and discard the collecting liquid. Rub the remaining cure mix over the moose and return it to the resealable bag. Place in the refrigerator for an additional 7 days, again turning it every couple of days.

After the second curing, remove the meat from the refrigerator and rinse thoroughly under cold water to remove any remaining spices. Pat dry with paper towel. Place the meat on a rack set on a baking sheet. Leave uncovered at room temperature for a few hours.

Tie the meat with butcher's twine along the length so that it can be hung. Hang the meat (ideally at 15°C with 60 to 70% humidity) for about 3 weeks. The meat should feel firm on the outside and silky smooth when sliced. For safe curing practices, be sure that your cured meat has lost 30% of its green weight before consuming.

Once cured, slice the meat up completely and vacuum-pack it in small portions. Or vacuum-pack it whole and just reseal it after you use part of it. If you do not vacuum-pack it, the meat will continue to dry out and will become as hard as stone. I have sometimes let this happen for use as a grated flavour enhancer over pasta, in soups, and on salads.

To serve, slice paper-thin and drizzle with olive oil and lemon juice. You can also serve it with shaved Parmigiano-Reggiano, greens, and thin slices of baguette. **LM**

Moose & Goose

Every year our family would get a moose licence and every year the moose would be processed the same way. I was not fond of the way it was done, so I began to process and package a quarter of moose myself into what I thought I would use throughout the year. In the beginning, I cut most of the meat into cubes and packaged them in 2-pound bags to be frozen for making moose stew or ground for burgers or sausages.

That changed when I started curing meat. My younger son loves bologna, but I hate buying it. So why not make my own? It was a success. He loved it. The next logical step was a mortadella. That worked out, too. My lovely neighbours, John and Jane Green, give me gooseberries from their garden every year. Adding the tang of the berries to the savoury meat is a natural fit. Now I make this every year; it's great with a salad for a quick no-fuss supper with a salad or as part of a boil-up breakfast. **MT**

Cod boudain blanc and moose mortadella
with gooseberries.

MOOSE MORTADELLA WITH GOOSEBERRIES

2.5 lb (1150 g) moose meat

1.25 lb (525 g) pork

0.5 lb (225 g) pork belly or bacon

2 tbsp (35 g) sea salt

*0.25 tsp (1.8 g) Prague powder cure #1

2 tbsp (60 g) powdered milk

2 tbsp (47 g) spruce tip syrup (maple syrup is a great substitute)

2 tsp (5.0 g) ground coriander

0.5 tsp (1.5 g) ground mace

1.5 tsp (4.5 g) ground white pepper

2 tsp (5.0 g) garlic powder

1 tsp (2.0 g) paprika

Pinch ground allspice

1 tsp (4 g) whole black peppercorns (optional)

½ cup (60 g) gooseberries (fresh or frozen)

Divide the pork fat (pork belly or bacon) in half. Cut one into ¼-inch dice. Chill and set aside for later. Grind the moose, pork, and the other half of the fat through the medium plate of a meat grinder. Add salt and cure, mix well, then refrigerate for several hours.

Add the powdered milk, spruce tip syrup, and remaining spices, except the whole peppercorns, to the ground meat and blend thoroughly. While keeping this mixture chilled, regrind through a small plate.

Add the reserved cubed fat, whole peppercorns, and gooseberries, mixing gently to disperse in the meat paste.

Press the meat mixture into a greased baking container (bread pans work well). Be sure to remove all the air pockets. Place a heavy ovenproof object on top of the meat to press the meat down while cooking—a similar-sized baking container with a weight in it works well.

Place a pot large enough to hold the baking container on the stovetop and half fill with water. Bring the water to a boil. Place the meat-filled container in the pot; check that the height of the water reaches just above the level of the meat. Poach until the meat reaches an internal temperature of 155°F. This will take 2 to 3 hours. When the meat reaches this temperature, place the container in an ice bath to cool it down quickly. Chill overnight in the refrigerator before removing from the container and slicing. **MT**

* Cure amount is lower than recommended but is **only** added for colour and texture. This sausage is meant to be thoroughly cooked to a high temperature (165°F), not just smoked. If you want to smoke this, the cure amount needs to be adjusted per weight of the meat in proper proportions (1 level teaspoon of Cure #1 for 5 pounds of meat). If you want a smoky flavour without smoking the meat, use smoked bacon as your fat or add a liquid smoke product.

COD BOUDAIN BLANC

I love fishcakes and I love being able to take them on a trip. Unfortunately, the cakes don't like it. I always made them up in advance and then froze them to take in a cooler but as they defrosted, they would get smashed up. I needed something a little more pack-worthy. I had purchased a spring-loaded pressure plate charcuterie poacher called a "ham maker." It seemed to be a perfect instrument to use to make a round of sausage that could be sliced into portions about the same size as a fish cake. A recipe for a sausage called boudain blanc was the starting point for my experimentation. Instead of making it with pork or chicken, I made a boudain blanc with salt cod. This is the delicious result.

If you do not have a ham maker, use any tall heatproof dish or bread pan, or make a tube with multiple layers of plastic wrap tied off tightly at both ends.

½ lb soaked, cooked, and flaked salt cod (If you are using corned cod, there is no need to soak it)

½ lb pork, finely ground

½ lb cooked basmati or other rice

1 large onion, chopped

Butter

Olive oil

Vermouth, whiskey, or Newfoundland Distillery Aquavit

Egg whites

Cream

SPICE MIXTURE: I use black pepper, savory, paprika, and a few ground juniper berries.

Caramelize the chopped onions in a frying pan with oil and a little butter. When the onions become golden, deglaze the pan with a small splash of your spirit of choice. Combine the fish, pork, rice, caramelized onions, and spices. Add just enough egg whites and cream to bind the ingredients together. The mixture should be tacky.

Spray the ham-maker cylinder with nonstick spray and fill with the meat mixture, making sure it is packed tightly with no air pockets. Poach in a water bath up to the level of the meat in the container until the internal temperature reaches 155°F.

Cool completely in the refrigerator before removing the salt cod mixture from the container.

I cut the finished boudain blanc in 1-inch-thick slices, lay them flat on a tray lined with parchment paper, freeze, then vacuum-seal. These are fully cooked, so they just need to be reheated in a frying pan. A great addition to your next camping or canoeing trip. **MT**

Mind the Gap

AUGUST 28, 2020. We arrive at Flat Bay at 12:50 p.m. It's a grey blustery day. We get out of the truck and look over the bluff to see the wind crashing the salt water over the left side of a long spit of land that eventually meets up with an island off our island far on the horizon. Lori looks at me: "We're going out there?!"

I nod and with a big smile on my face I start to get ready for departure to one of my favourite places—Sandy Point. My two sons are helping us carry gear over for our overnight cooking excursion. We had to get going; the tide was low and typically you can only access this island when it is. When the tide is high, "The Gap" or connection point to the island disappears underwater, leaving you marooned until the next low tide.

We arrive, set up camp, and start preparing for a night of cooking. This recipe was on the menu. One problem: we need sweet gale. Lori saw lots of it on the way to our departure point on the mainland, but there seemed to be a lack of it on the island.

The island has so many different ecosystems, though, I was pretty sure I could find some. I hopped in the side by side and left Lori behind, alone. After half an hour or more, I finally found one small little outcrop of the bush next to a bog. I gathered it and texted Lori a picture of the plant.

My phone dings back with a message:

Omg! You're something else!
Hurry back before I'm carried off by fairies!

No fairies carried her away. Only one of the local island foxes paid us a visit while we were making this over an open fire. I think it was the smell of the sweet gale basting the moose that drew him in. **MT**

Sweet gale.

MOOSE TENDERLOIN AND CHANTERELLES

½ lb moose tenderloin
approximately 8" long,
cleaned of all silver skin

2 thick slices bacon

3 tbsp salted butter

1 tsp sea salt

1 tsp pepper

2 tbsp oil

Handful of long woody
sweet gale sprigs (rosemary
or thyme sprigs can be
substituted)

Good splash of red wine
or beer

Season the tenderloin with salt and pepper on all sides. Over medium-high heat in a heavy-bottomed frying pan, fry the bacon slices for a few minutes to release the oil.

With the bacon still in the pan, sear the tenderloin well on all sides. Just before you have finished searing, add 2 tablespoons butter to the pan. With the sweet gale sprigs, baste the meat with the melted butter by swirling the herb through the butter and over the meat. Continue brushing the meat with the buttered herbs for 3 to 5 minutes. This will give you a rare temperature meat. If you like your meat more well done, baste for longer.

Once the desired temperature has been reached, remove the tenderloin from the pan and let it rest, uncovered, for 5 minutes. In the empty but still hot frying pan, throw in the remaining 1 tablespoon butter, a good splash of red wine or beer, and 1 tablespoon chopped fresh sweet gale. Let reduce by half. For more sauce, add more liquid of your choice. Slice meat in ½-inch slices. Spread the sauce and fried herbs over the meat and serve. **LM**

Don't ever throw out your Parmesan cheese rinds. I store mine in the freezer and pull them out any time I am doing a low and slow dish. The rind creates a beautiful depth of flavour in all kinds of simmering pots of soups and sauces but will not melt, so it can be removed before serving.

I always make this sauce in bulk and then freeze in meal-sized containers. After all, I would rather make the one mess and enjoy it several times. The addition of red wine, Parmesan cheese, rinds, and cream creates something maybe a little different than your usual sauce. Enjoy.

MOOSE BOLOGNESE

3 tbsp olive oil

4 slices bacon (2-inch chunk of fatback can be substituted)

1 lb moose meat, cut in 1-inch chunks

Sea salt

2 cups onion, chopped

1 cup carrot, minced

1 cup celery, minced

¼ cup wild dried mushrooms

¼ cup tomato paste

1 can (28 oz) crushed tomatoes

1 can (20 oz) diced tomatoes

1 can (14 oz) tomato sauce

1 cup red wine, the bolder the better

1 cup Parmesan, freshly grated

1 bunch parsley, chopped

1 palm-sized piece of Parmesan cheese rind

½ cup whipping cream

Heat olive oil in a large Dutch oven over medium-high heat. Render out the bacon. Brown the moose well. Take your time and do this in batches. You want the meat to brown, not steam. Salt the meat sparingly as it cooks. When all of the meat is browned, set aside.

In the same pot, fry the onion, carrot, and celery until soft. Add the mushrooms and stir occasionally until the vegetables begin to brown and caramelize. Return the meat to the pot and mix well. Add more oil, if needed.

In a small bowl, whisk together the tomato paste and wine. Add to the meat mixture and stir well. Turn the heat to high, then add the crushed and diced tomatoes plus the cheese rind. Mix well, bring to a boil and reduce the heat to a bare simmer with only a few bubbles coming to the surface. After 2 hours, add the cream. Cover and let this simmer for up to another 2 hours, stirring occasionally. **LM**

FIRE-ROASTED GROUSE

1 whole grouse, plucked
but not skinned

BASTING LIQUID

1 cup water

2 slices yellow onion

1 clove garlic, chopped

1 tbsp salt

Over an open fire method

Cut two 2-foot-long alder branches approximately ½-inch thick, with the leaves still attached. Skin the bark off the ends of each branch and sharpen the ends. Skewer the grouse with the alder branches through each breast and upper thigh.

Create a hot coal bed by letting the fire burn down until there is no flame but only red coals. You should be able to hold your hand over the coals for 3 or 4 seconds. Push the sharpened end of the skewers into the ground next to the bed of coals so that the grouse is close to the coals.

Combine the basting liquid ingredients in a heavy pot or frying pan on the coals. Roast the grouse for approximately 45 minutes to 1 hour (depending on the heat of the coals), basting throughout. A great basting brush is a handful of short alder twigs with the leaves still attached. The grouse will be done when the internal temperature reaches 165°F.

Smoker method

Set the smoker to 300°F and load with your wood of choice. Alder is a wonderful pairing for poultry, especially grouse. Smoke the grouse for approximately 1 to 2 hours, basting throughout. Check the meat until the internal temperature reaches 165°F. **LM**

Treasured Game

These birds may be the most treasured game in all of Newfoundland. Traditionally, ptarmigan were simply oven roasted, stuffed with a bread stuffing, and served with gravy. I don't remember them much from my childhood. I grew up in Bauline and the terrain wasn't "birding ground," and Dad didn't do any upland bird hunting as such. However, in the past few years ptarmigan have become one of my absolute favourite game meats.

In 2019, I was selected to take part in "Canada's Kitchen 2019: Meet the country's next top chefs," an annual article in the *Globe and Mail*. I wanted to showcase our beautiful wild game meat and share with Canadians the quality of the amazing resources we have here. This very simple dish allows the flavour of the ptarmigan to be enjoyed with fall cranberries—the rich meat with the tart berries are a great combination. **LM**

PTARMIGAN WITH WILD GREENS AND SAUTÉED CRANBERRIES

1 breast of ptarmigan
(duck breast can be
substituted, but remove skin)

Sea salt

Black pepper, freshly ground

4 tbsp butter, salted, divided

2 tbsp olive oil

¼ cup frozen cranberries

½ tsp sweet gale
or fresh rosemary

¼ cup red wine

Salt and pepper the meat well on both sides. Heat the frying pan to medium high and add 2 tablespoons butter and 2 tablespoons olive oil. Give the meat a quick sear, turning just once, 1 to 2 minutes per side for ptarmigan (2 to 3 minutes per side for duck). Remove the seared meat from the pan and set aside on a plate to rest while you prepare the cranberries.

Reserve a few cranberries to add later. Add the rest of the berries to the frying pan. Season with a pinch of pepper. Add the sweet gale and wine. Bring to a boil just for a moment. Break the cranberries with a fork. Whisk in 2 tablespoons butter and let the sauce reduce by half.

To plate, slice the meat thinly against the grain and arrange slices flat on a plate. Drizzle with a few tablespoons of the cranberry sauce, add some sliced berries, drizzle with olive oil, and sprinkle on a little sea salt and fresh cracked pepper. **LM**

WILD DUCK SLIDERS

1 wild duck (do not buy wild ducks, you will end up with a visit from a wildlife officer) or 10 oz deboned meat

1 tbsp fat, rendered from duck skin, store-bought duck fat, or butter

1 tsp orange zest, finely grated

1 tsp cranberries, finely grated

6 small brioche buns, toasted

6 lettuce leaves

MARINADE

¼ cup Worcestershire sauce (must be Lea & Perrins)

1 tsp fish sauce

1 tsp toasted sesame oil

2 tbsp lime juice, freshly squeezed

¼ tsp your favourite hot sauce

2 tbsp runny honey

1 tbsp green onion, thinly sliced

2 tsp ginger, finely grated

½ clove garlic, grated

Debone the duck breasts and legs. The bones make excellent stock and can be frozen to be used at a later time. Reserve the skin; you can render the oils out in a frying pan for frying the burgers. Using the breasts and the legs without the skin, the total weight of the duck meat should be about 10 ounces. Chop the meat to a fine mince.

Combine all marinade ingredients. Mix 4 tablespoons liquid marinade with the meat and refrigerate.

To make the tomato chutney, coat the tomatoes in the olive oil, salt, pepper, and garlic. Place the tomatoes in a shallow pan and oven-roast at 450°F until slightly charred. Remove from the oven and hand cut or place tomatoes in a countertop blender to achieve a rough chop. In a medium saucepan, combine the brown sugar, vinegar, and anise. Bring to a boil to dissolve the sugar. Reduce the heat to simmer, add the onion and tomatoes, and cook until the liquid has reduced enough so that when it is stirred you can easily see the bottom of the pot.

ROASTED TOMATO CHUTNEY

1 lb fresh tomatoes

3 to 4 tbsp olive oil

Salt and pepper

1 garlic clove, smashed

½ cup onion, chopped

½ cup brown sugar

¼ cup red wine vinegar

2 star anise

ROASTED TOMATO MAYONNAISE

3 tbsp chutney

3 tbsp your favourite mayonnaise

COLESLAW

1½ cups white or red cabbage, hand sliced or shredded

¼ cup red onion, thinly sliced

1 tsp white sugar

¼ tsp salt

3 tsp red wine vinegar

⅓ cup cilantro, chopped

¼ tsp your favourite hot sauce

To make the tomato mayonnaise, combine 3 table-spoons chutney with 3 tablespoons mayo plus a pinch of salt.

For the coleslaw, combine all the ingredients and macerate with your hands for several minutes until it starts to break down. Set aside at room temperature.

Add the orange zest and cranberries to the duck meat. Divide the meat into six equal portions and shape each into a ball. Preheat a heavy-bottomed frying pan to medium low and add the fat. Add the balls to the hot oil and gently flatten each to approximately ¼ inch thick. Season lightly with a pinch of salt (top sides only). Cook each side for 1 to 2 minutes or until browned.

To assemble the sliders, top the bottom half of the toasted buns with a dollop of mayo, a little mound of coleslaw, a burger patty, lettuce, chutney, and the other half of the bun.

This recipe makes 6 sliders. The duck meat needs to be marinated the day before, so think ahead. You can also make the tomato chutney and mayo ahead of time.

BRIOCHE BUNS

I couldn't share a burger recipe without sharing a delicious bun to go with it. Don't hesitate to make this recipe to have with a big pot of soup in the winter or as a sandwich loaf when heading out into the woods.

A huge thank you to Alex Blagdon for this recipe. Alex is my cousin, a brilliant entrepreneur, chef, and the founder of the Alder Cottage cookery school, a place to share food, laughter, and good drinks. Alex runs Alder Cottage as an online cooking school, making it available to a global audience. **LM**

¼ cup milk

½ tbsp active dry yeast

3½ tbsp salted butter, melted

2 eggs

1½ cups all-purpose flour

2 tbsp sugar

1 tsp salt

1 egg (for egg wash)

Heat milk until just barely warm (100°F) and pour into a medium bowl. Add the yeast, melted butter, and eggs and lightly whisk together. In a separate bowl, whisk together the flour, sugar, and salt. Add the dry ingredients to the egg mixture and gently incorporate using your hands. When a rough dough has formed, turn it out onto a lightly floured surface. Knead the dough, adding flour as needed, until you get a nice firm bounce back when you give it a poke. This is what creates the lovely soft texture of the final bun. Put the dough in a clean bowl and place in a warm spot to rise until doubled in bulk.

Divide the dough into 3-ounce pieces. Tuck the edges under the bottom of the dough ball, cup your hand over it, and use a circular motion to roll the dough, tightening the skin and creating a smooth surface.

Oil the top of each bun lightly with a brush, cover with plastic wrap and cloth, and let rise until doubled in size.

Preheat the oven to 375°F. Mix one egg with 4 tablespoons water and use to brush the top of the buns. Sprinkle with sesame seeds if desired, and bake until golden, about 12 to 15 minutes.

Recipe by Alex Blagdon

WILD STARTER

The world is full of wild yeast, and "capturing" it over the years has been an exciting project for me—one that came in particularly handy in 2020 when Newfoundland seemed to run out of store-bought yeast. All hands were beside themselves, Mom included, until I reminded her that I had jars of starter (also known as mother yeast or sourdough starter) in the refrigerator.

Each of my starters has been named. *Hilda Maxine*, made from rhubarb, is one of my oldest. Mom once told me that Nan (her mother-in-law) wanted to name me Hilda Maxine. I have imagined my mother locking herself in a room and not coming out until my father told his mother that I would not be named that. *Margaret,* my first mushroom starter, was made from my wild mushroom powder collection and rye flour, and I was thrilled when she was a success. Zena is a black currant mother yeast, dark, bold, and strong. I was growing and cultivating yeast at quite a rate for friends and family during that time when yeast was scarce.

Wild yeast seems to "stick" better to some things than others. A few of my favourite plant products to cultivate wild yeast from are rhubarb, blueberries, and juniper berries. Fruit works particularly well, because the natural sugar in the fruit gives the wild yeast a kick-start early on, while others, like mushrooms, take a little more time. Of course, you could add sugar or honey.

MUSHROOM MOTHER YEAST

1 1-litre jar

¼ cup wild mushroom powder of your choice (I usually use a mix of hedgehogs and winter chanterelles)

¼ cup unbleached organic white flour

¼ cup unbleached organic rye flour

Unchlorinated water

Day 1:
Combine all ingredients in the jar and add just enough water to bring them together with the texture of a wet muffin batter. Cover with a damp cloth and leave on the counter overnight.

Day 2:
Add 1 heaping tablespoon of each flour and a little water and stir. Dampen the cloth again, cover the mix, and leave on the counter overnight.

Day 3:
Repeat Day 2 procedure.

You must not boil anything you are using to cultivate the yeast. This will kill the yeast. Do not use hot water in your mix.

I use organic, unbleached flour.

Day 4:

You should start seeing bubbles now! Discard half of the mix. (I know, it's hard to do. You could give it away or start another mother but, believe me, this whole hobby gets out of hand! You could also make Marsha's Wild Starter Crackers, page 157.) Add ¼ cup of both flours and more water to keep the mixture at the muffin batter consistency. Cover with the damp cloth and leave on the counter overnight.

Day 5:

Add 1 heaping tablespoon of each flour and a little water. Dampen the cloth again, cover the mix, and leave on the counter overnight. Tomorrow you will make bread.

Day 6:

It's bread making day! (See page 69 for Lori's Wild Caraway Rye Bread with Wild Starter recipe.)

Feeding and storing your mother

After you remove what you need to make your bread, you'll need to feed your mother yeast. Add 1 heaping tablespoon of each flour and a little water, cover with a damp cloth, and leave overnight. In the morning, cover the jar with a lid and put it in the refrigerator until two days before you want to use it.

Two days before you want to use your mother in a bread, start at Day 4 instructions. **LM**

WILD STARTER CRACKERS

I always hated throwing away sourdough bread starter every time I fed it; it's such a waste of something that I had worked so hard to keep alive and healthy. So I decided to start making crackers from the starter for my charcuterie boards. These are the perfect crispy and savoury cracker for special occasions or late-night refrigerator raids. You can use your active starter for a fluffier cracker or a "hungry" starter for a more sour flavour.

1 cup starter

1 cup flour (all-purpose or a blend of flours)

¼ cup fresh herbs of choice, or 2 tbsp dried

½ tsp sea salt

¼ cup oil (coconut oil, butter, or olive oil)

Olive oil, for brushing

¼ tsp garlic powder, optional

In a bowl, thoroughly combine the starter, flour, herbs, salt, and oil. Form into a large ball. Divide the ball into two. Shape each half into a patty-like rectangle about ½ inch thick. Cover with plastic wrap or parchment paper and refrigerate for at least 30 minutes or up to 2 hours.

Preheat the oven to 350°F. Place each dough patty on a piece of floured parchment paper and roll out with a floured rolling pin until the dough is a thin sheet, about ¹⁄₁₆ inch thick. Lightly brush the dough sheets with olive oil and sprinkle with sea salt. Cut the dough using a pasta cutter, pastry cutter, or knife into 1- to 2-inch squares. Using a fork, poke each dough square several times. Transfer each parchment sheet to a baking sheet and bake for 20 to 25 minutes. Rotate the baking sheets halfway through to help them bake evenly.

Transfer the baked crackers to a cooling rack. When completely cool, store the crackers in an airtight container. **MT**

RABBIT LIVER PATÉ

There is no reason why every part of the valuable wild animal you have managed to procure should not be used to its fullest—that includes the offal or organ meats. If I did not tell you what the delicious, silky, savoury spread was on the charcuterie plate, you would eat it and ask for the recipe. Here it is.

Don't waste anything. In many cultures, including ours, this is a delicacy that can only be obtained during a small window in time. Savour it to its fullest. It also makes a pretty fancy gift for the foodie in your life!

8 oz rabbit liver, cleaned, sinew removed, and cut into chunks

2 tbsp + ¼ cup unsalted butter

2 shallots, peeled and finely diced

1 clove garlic, sliced

1 sprig fresh thyme, leaves removed from the stem and finely chopped

1 tsp fresh parsley, finely chopped

¼ cup Newman's port

Salt and pepper

3 tbsp whipping cream

Melt 2 tablespoons butter in a small frying pan until bubbling. Add the onion and garlic and fry gently for 5 minutes until golden brown and soft. Add the liver and cook for 2 minutes before adding the port, parsley, thyme, salt, and pepper. Stir while burning off the alcohol from the port and reduce the amount of liquid by half. Remove from the heat, and leave for 10 minutes to cool.

Place everything in a food processor and blend until smooth. Using a fine sieve, pass the paté through with a spatula to screen out any solids. In a separate bowl, whisk the cream until stiff peaks form. Gently fold the cream into the paté, until mixed. Pour the paté into a storage container with a lid. Cover the surface with ¼ cup melted butter to prevent oxidation or a skin forming on the surface.

Serve at room temperature but refrigerate in a sealed container until use. **MT**

Rabbit Wings

While growing up, we would occasionally drive to Deer Lake from our home in Pasadena. Along the way, we'd pass through a little town called St. Jude's. Without fail, someone would have a sign up next to the highway. In summer, it would read "Worms for Sale"; in winter, "Rabbits $5 a Pair." Sometimes they would even have the rabbits out on the road next to the sign with a jar for payment. I believe it was mostly kids snaring rabbits for a bit of pocket money. For any youngster interested in hunting, snaring rabbits was an introduction to that world before they were old enough to be safely taught how to handle a firearm.

This recipe is derived from the raw-packed bottling method my father discovered. Before the advent of refrigeration, meats were salt-cured to preserve them. *Corning* is an Anglo-Saxon term for dry cured meats that were rubbed with salt pellets similar in size to corn. The process evolved and wet curing or brining was also developed. The term *corned* is sometimes still used for both processes. This recipe uses a brine, but instead of curing the meat first for seven days in a brine and then processing it in bottles, you corn and pressure can the rabbit in one easy step. Simply wait one week before eating for the full curing process to be complete.

Do not discard rabbit carcasses after deboning. You can use these for the rabbit reduction recipe (see page 165). If you do not want loose spices in the finished jars of rabbit, place them in a sachet to be removed when you are ready to bottle. Adding a chicken wing tip to each jar adds bone gelatin to the liquid in the jar and boosts the flavour of the stock.

All meat and meat products must be canned in a pressure canner. A water bath method is not sufficient to safely preserve the contents. **MT**

BOTTLED RABBIT WITH THE WING

6 to 8 lb rabbit meat, deboned and cut in 1-inch chunks

16 cups water

2 cups non-iodized salt

2½ tsp Prague Powder #2

3 tbsp pickling spice

½ cup brown sugar

1 chicken wing tip for each jar

PICKLING SPICE

2 tbsp whole mustard

1 tbsp juniper berries

2 tsp whole coriander seeds

1 tsp red pepper flakes

10 dried sweet gale leaves, crushed

1 tsp ground ginger

½ tsp ground allspice

Combine all ingredients except the rabbit in a non-reactive saucepan and bring to a boil. Reduce the heat but keep the brine hot.

Prepare the pressure canner by filling it with water and bringing it to a simmer. Sterilize the jars in a hot water bath, in the oven, or by washing them in the dishwasher and removing them while they are still hot. Put the cut-up pieces of rabbit in the sterilized, heated jars. Add one chicken wing tip in the centre of each jar. Cover the meat with hot brine, leaving 1¼ inches of headspace. Remove any air bubbles, wipe the rim of the bottle, and then place the heated lid on top. Screw on the ring hand-tight and place each bottle in the canner.

For ½ litre (500 ml) bottles, process for 75 minutes at 10 pounds in a weighted pressure canner or 11 pounds in a dial gauge pressure canner. For 1-litre bottles, process for 90 minutes at 10 pounds in a weighted pressure canner or 11 pounds in a dial gauge pressure canner.

Once the rabbit is processed and the jars have cooled, store in a pantry for 7 days before opening them. **MT**

RABBIT STOCK

2 rabbits, cleaned

Oil (enough to cover the bottom of the pan)

2 tbsp butter

1 stalk of celery

1 large carrot

4 bay leaves

6 juniper berries

½ tsp peppercorns

2 onions, rough chopped, peel on

2 cups red wine (merlot or other heavy wine)

4 cups water

Heat oil and butter in a Dutch oven or roasting pan on the stovetop. Sear the rabbit carcasses on all sides. Make sure it is browed all over. Add the celery, carrot, bay leaves, juniper berries, peppercorns, and onion. Continue to fry until the vegetables have browned a little. Add the wine and water. Tightly cover, and bake at 350°F for 2 hours.

Remove from the oven and pull all the meat off the rabbits and reserve. This can be frozen or used right away. Strain the liquid into a saucepan, place it on the top of the stove, and reduce until you have about 2 cups of rich, dark stock. Discard the strained vegetables and bones.

Pour the stock into ice cube trays and freeze. Once frozen, wrap each cube in parchment paper and place in freezer bags. Use within 6 months. **LM**

WILD RABBIT ROULADE

I created this dish just because I like improving my knife skills and I had a lot of rabbit in the freezer. This would be great served over rabbit risotto (page 224).

1 large wild rabbit

1 large carrot, peeled

1 large parsnip, peeled

1 tbsp dried sweet gale

3 thin slices of bacon

Sea salt and alder pepper

2 cups stock

1 cup red wine

Lay the rabbit cavity side up on a cutting board. Dislocate the legs and arms so that it lays flat. With a sharp paring knife, start making shallow cuts at the ribcage, revealing meat until you get to the spine. Take your time; it is okay if you cut through the meat. Once you reach the spine, use the knife to gently reveal the meat around the spine until it is freed. Repeat the same procedure on the other side of the ribcage until you free the entire spine and ribcage from the meat.

Place the spine and ribcage in a shallow roasting pan and roast in a 375°F oven for 45 minutes while you prepare the rest of the roulade.

Remove the front and back legs from the rabbit's body. Reserve for a later use or debone to add to the meat you will be rolling. Place the deboned rabbit body on a cutting board. Season the meat with salt, pepper, and sweet gale. Lay the bacon on top of the seasonings. Using a vegetable peeler, make long strips of carrot and parsnip and lay lengthways over the middle of the meat. Roll up the boneless rabbit meat and tie with cooking twine.

Once the ribcage and spine have finished roasting, remove from the oven. Take the bones out of the pan and replace with the rabbit roll (the roulade). Add 1 cup stock and 1 cup wine to the roasting pan. Cover the pan and reduce the oven temperature to 250°F.

Roast the roulade for 2½ hours. Check halfway through to make sure it isn't dry, adding stock as needed to keep ½ inch of liquid in the pan. After 2½ hours, remove from the oven and let the roulade sit until cool enough to handle. Wrap the roulade in plastic wrap to prevent it from drying out. Refrigerate until chilled through and firm enough to slice. Scrape any brown bits from the bottom of the pan and reserve with the pan juices. This liquid can be strained if desired.

To serve, thinly slice the roulade, then gently reheat in a pan until warmed through. Meanwhile, reheat the cooking liquid with a splash of wine. Plate and spoon some of the cooking juices over the top. **MT**

All Hands Arse Up

At one point in the preparation of this book, I turned to Marsha and said that we really should call the fall section "all hands arse up"—and anyone from Newfoundland would know why.

"All hands arse up" perfectly depicts the fall of year here and, more specifically, the berry season. I cannot recall how many times over the years I have been asked by travellers why there are so many cars parked along the highways and why are the hills so full of people. To which I would respond "oh, you mean, why are all hands all arse up? They're all berry picking." I would go on to explain the traditions of berry picking, and how important it is to fill our pantries and freezers with berries for the winter.

Today, many of our refrigerators are filled with fresh fruit and berries year-round, however, this was not the case in my mom's time. Many will tell you that berry season brought some of the most exciting times of the year—the only time they ever saw fresh berries was when the land provided them. Berry season started in June with bakeapples (cloudberries), then the tiny delicious wild strawberries in July. It was August before the blueberries came, followed by the partridgeberries (lingonberries) in late October. Cranberries were the last to be picked. Although there were others, these were the most important berries harvested to make jams and jellies, and to freeze for baking throughout the year.

You'll hear many a seasoned berry picker say that you have to wait for the first good frost to pick the partridgeberries because the frost drives the worms out of them. While the berries are not full of worms—only once in my berry picking life did I ever see a worm in a berry— but it's true that the lingonberry fruitworm is laid by a small moth that burrows into the berry, and it is true that you can avoid encountering the fruitworm if you hold off harvesting until after the front. My advice? Listen to the wisdom of the berry pickers before you. _LM_

CHAGA TEA

The smaller the chaga pieces are, the better, so go for marble-sized pieces or powder if you can. I use a blender or a box-style cheese grater to break up the chaga.

Place 3.5 oz (100 g) chaga and 4 cups water in a saucepan and bring to a boil. Simmer 4 to 6 hours, until the water has reduced to 2 cups. If more water is needed before the simmering time is complete, add a little at a time, keeping the water amount to about 2 cups. Once the chaga has finished simmering, strain the liquid into a jar. Cover and refrigerate for up to 4 weeks.

To make chaga tea, add about ¼ cup reduced chaga liquid to 1 cup boiled water; experiment with the strength to suit your own tastes. I often add a 1-inch piece of vanilla bean or a cinnamon stick to the simmering chaga. Play with it and find a nice mix for yourself. **LM**

PARTRIDGEBERRY CHUTNEY

Many times I have asked the people of this province to share their recipes, stories, and preservation techniques. I have created vivid images from these stories of old wooden barrels, full of berries submerged in water, in barns and cellars, and scenes in which women trek to the barn in the winter, break the ice that had formed on top of the barrel, and scoop out the precious partridgeberries to bring into the home for the family.

This chutney was created to accompany a seal loin meal prepared aboard the *Adventure Canada* Newfoundland circumnavigation in 2018. Those trying seal for the first time are often wary and I felt it best to give them something with a nice acid to cut through the strong taste. Much to my surprise, as I walked around the dining room that evening, I saw that every plate had been cleaned. Oftentimes it's our own apprehensions about our traditional foods and meals that we project onto others. It's moments like this I find very affirming and I am proud that I have given so much of my time to our food.

1 small onion, diced

2 cups apples, peeled and diced

½ tsp salt

Zest and juice of 1 orange

¼ cup apple cider vinegar

2 cups partridgeberries

1 tsp nutmeg

½ tsp cardamom

½ tsp ground cloves

2 tbsp brown sugar

3 juniper berries, ground

Add all ingredients to a small saucepan and simmer for 1 hour. Stir the mixture occasionally as it can stick quite quickly. Once it is done, give it a taste and adjust the sugar or vinegar to your taste. **LM**

Christmas Tradition

I t's not Christmas till Mom takes raisin bread out of the oven. I could argue that the Christmas Eve ham is the beginning of the seasonal celebration, but all the bread is made weeks ahead of the ham, so let's give the moment to the bread. That's the smell of Christmas, that's home, and that's what it's all about for me. Growing up, there was never any shortage of homemade bread, cookies, raisin buns, partridgeberry loaves, and too many more to mention. Mom's a fine baker and we were the lucky recipients of all that love.

MOM'S RAISIN BREAD

2 cups boiling water

½ cup fancy molasses

1 tbsp sea salt

½ cup shortening

1 tbsp cinnamon

2 cups lukewarm water

1 tsp brown sugar

2 tbsp traditional yeast

9½ cups unbleached flour

2 cups Thompson raisins

Mix the boiling water, molasses, salt, shortening, and cinnamon in a large bowl. Let the mixture cool to lukewarm before continuing.

Mix the lukewarm water, brown sugar, and yeast in a small bowl and let sit for 20 minutes to let the yeast bloom. Add 1 to 1½ cups of flour in the yeast bowl and beat with a wooden spoon until smooth. When the molasses mixture has cooled, add the yeast mixture and stir until incorporated. Add 8 cups flour to the large bowl, 2 cups at a time. Before the mixture gets too dry, add the raisins. Then continue adding the remaining flour, as required, with your hands.

Knead well, until a soft dough forms. Turn the dough out onto a floured table or counter. Knead for 5 to 7 minutes until smooth. You cannot overwork this dough. Place the kneaded dough in a greased bowl and cover with plastic wrap and a tea towel. Place the bowl in a warm place to rise until doubled in bulk, about 1 to 2 hours.

When the dough has risen, punch it down and divide it into three and shape into loaves. Place dough in bread pans. Place the pans in a warm place, covered with a tea towel, and let rise again before baking.

Preheat the oven to 375°F. Once the dough has sufficiently risen in the pans, gently place the loaves in the oven to bake for 40 minutes, or until the loaf sounds hollow when tapped on the bottom. Turn the loaves out of the pans and place on a cooling rack. Butter the tops of each for a softer loaf. **LM**

Makes 3 loaves.

pantry to plate

JANUARY

FEBRUARY

MARCH

"Cold enough to skin ya."

— Shirley Butler,
Pouch Cove

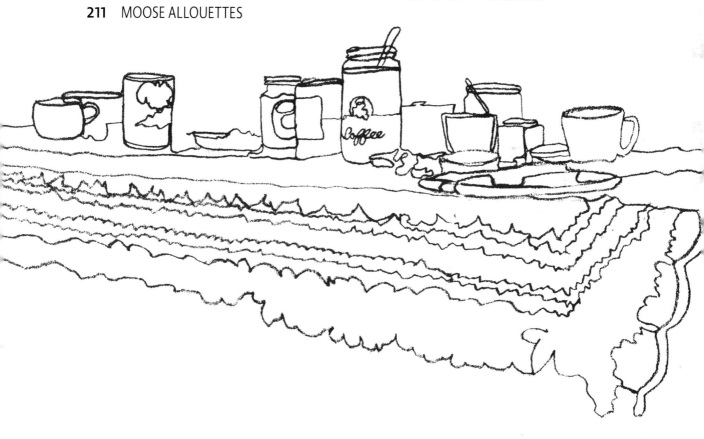

WILD GAME BREAKFAST PATTIES

½ lb frozen goose, duck,
or ptarmigan breast

½ lb frozen smoky bacon

2 tbsp fresh thyme, sage,
and/or sweet gale

2 tbsp maple syrup

1 tsp salt

½ tsp pepper

1 clove garlic, grated

Partially thaw the bacon and game meat (it is very important the meat is still half-frozen). Cut the meat and bacon into 1.5- to 2-inch chunks. Place the chunks in a food processor with the rest of the ingredients and pulse until well combined. It may take 15 to 20 pulses to get to a workable, tacky consistency. You want the patties to hold together and not crumble apart when forming and cooking.

Make 12 meatballs from the mixture and flatten each to ½ inch thick. Heat a medium frying pan to a medium heat and fry the patties on each side for 3 minutes. Let sit only 2 to 3 minutes before serving. The patties dry out if they sit too long.

Makes 12 small patties.

Make 12. If you make fewer than 12, the patties are too big and dry out before they are cooked. Ensure that each patty is flat and even all around, not thin on the edges and fat in the middle. Serve the patties right away, when they are at their most juicy and delicious.

CLARENCE'S MOLASSES BUNS

If there's anyone else in the house when you make these, you had better make another batch right away—they will disappear in mere seconds while they are warm. My mother gave me this recipe from my Uncle Clarence. They are addictive. **MT**

½ cup milk

1 egg

1 cup molasses

1 tsp cinnamon

2 tsp baking soda

½ cup sugar

1 cup butter, melted

4 cups all-purpose flour

1 cup raisins, optional

Combine the milk, egg, molasses, cinnamon, and baking soda in a microwave-safe bowl. Add the sugar and butter. Stir well. Microwave for 40 seconds to soften but do not melt the butter.

Add the flour and the raisins, if using, and mix well. Using a tablespoon or ice cream scoop, place large scoops of batter onto a parchment-lined baking sheet, 3 inches apart. Bake at 350°F for 25 to 30 minutes.

Recipe by Clarence Lucas

Clarence's Molasses Buns.

MOM'S TEA BUNS

For the love of buns! I can't tell you how many of these were whipped up by Mom in my childhood. So many laughs, so many cups of tea around the table, and so many buns carried off in the woods with us in the winter. We'd warm them in foil by the fire or toast them over the old rack we'd left behind and hung from a tree at our favourite ice-fishing hole. Slathered with butter and enjoyed with a cuppa in the woods, there's nothing quite like it.

The raisins are optional. As children, we often picked out the raisins. Mom would sometimes make them without the raisins and today I make them without the raisins for my kids too. **LM**

---

3 cups all-purpose flour

4 tsp baking powder

½ tsp salt

½ cup white sugar

1 cup butter

1 cup raisins

¾ cup milk

1 egg

Preheat the oven to 425°F. Place the flour, baking powder, salt, and sugar in a large bowl wide enough to get your hands in. Add in the butter with your hands: pinch the butter into marble-sized pieces, then rub your hands together until you have worked the butter in evenly and the mixture resembles a crumble. Add the raisins and gently mix into the rough dough.

In a separate bowl, lightly whisk together the egg and milk; reserve ¼ cup for an egg wash over the top of the buns. Add the rest of the milk and egg mixture to the dough. Gently bring together the dough with a light touch (patting, not kneading). If the dough is too dry and won't come together, drizzle in a little milk until it does.

Turn the dough onto a floured surface and pat down to a 1 inch thickness. Dust with a little flour. Cut rounds from the dough with a glass or large cookie cutter. Lay each round on a cookie sheet lined with parchment paper or a non-stick baking mat. Brush each bun with the reserved milk-egg mixture. Bake for 20 minutes or until golden brown.

Recipe by Shirley Butler

Mom's Tea Buns.

CREAM OF MUSHROOM SOUP

2 tbsp salted butter

2 tbsp olive oil

1 medium onion, chopped

2 large cloves garlic, chopped

1 5 oz package fresh
mushrooms, roughly chopped

1 cup of your favorite
fresh wild mushrooms,
roughly chopped

¼ cup sherry

2 cups unsalted stock

1 cup whole milk

2 tbsp wild dehydrated
mushroom powder, optional

1 can Fussell's cream

½ cup celery, chopped

¼ cup fresh parsley, chopped

¼ cup wild leeks or
green onion, chopped

1 tbsp fresh thyme

½ tsp pepper

1 tsp salt

In a large pot, heat the olive oil and butter over medium heat. Add the chopped onion and garlic and sauté for 10 minutes until lightly brown. Add all the chopped mushrooms to the onions and sauté for an additional 10 minutes. Deglaze the pot with the sherry, scraping the bottom of the pot to release all of the browned bits. Add the stock and simmer for 10 minutes.

Add the whole milk and mushroom powder. Simmer for another 10 minutes. Add the cream, celery, parsley, leeks, thyme, pepper, and salt. Blend the soup with an immersion blender or a countertop blender to your preferred consistency—fine or chunky.

This is not meant to be a thick soup. Reheat and serve with a lightly oiled toasted crusty bread rubbed with a fresh garlic clove. **LM**

JIGGS' DINNER SOUP

We have all done it—put an extra potato and few extra carrots plus that one extra turnip in the pot just in case someone drops by for supper. And at the end of a big Sunday supper, you have a pile of leftovers to pack away in the fridge. I love leftover veggies chopped up and fried for hash the next day. Sometimes I like that more than the first go-round. But if you are in the mood for a change, this is a great lunch for the week ahead. Don't forget to save a few cups of pot liquor; combine equal parts of pot liquor and water to make a wonderful stock for this soup.

5 cups leftover vegetables (including pease pudding) from Jiggs' dinner, chopped

5 cups stock

1 onion, chopped

1 tbsp oil

Salt meat (optional)

Sauté the chopped onion in a small frying pan in the oil until golden. In the meantime, add the stock to a large pot over medium heat. Once the onion is cooked and the stock is thoroughly heated, add the vegetables and pease pudding to the pot. Heat everything thoroughly and blend until smooth with an immersion blender or in batches in a countertop blender. If the soup is too thick, add additional stock. Adjust the seasoning as needed.

I often add any leftover salt meat too. **LM**

The Joy of Wild Mussels

W ild mussels are just one of the amazing goodies from the sea in Newfoundland. Many of us remember long summer days spent with family and friends boiling up mussels on the beach.

When we talk to locals who live near popular mussel beds, they usually say the same thing: "Mussels are not like they used to be." I picked mussels as a child down in Dildo Bay and even I can say the same, just 30 years later. I can't claim to know the reason and it seems that many don't. When I do manage to get some wild mussels these days, they are all the more special.

A few months ago, a fella named Ernest from out around Norman's Cove emailed to ask if I wanted a feed of wild mussels. (That kind of random contact is not unusual. I get everything from "I heard you're the girl that picks stuff off the beach" to "I'm coming by to drop a feed of fresh fish off.") This email continued: "I got a bag tied onto the wharf and if my brother doesn't get to them before me, I'll bring them in next week ... bring a big bucket." Any good mussel picker knows that you have to get the mussels up off the ocean floor and let them purge out the sand for a few days so you don't get a mouthful of grit when you eat them.

I met Ernest and his wife in a parking lot. He hauled out a huge homemade bucket cut from the bottom of a plastic barrel. What the hell was I going to do with 25 pounds of mussels? "My God, Ernest, keep some of them for yourself," was my comment. He came back with "Get your bucket!"

We've all been told that there are five senses, though I've come to learn there are many more, and in Newfoundland, the most important one is a sense of humour.

Ernest poured out the mussels into my big tub and started laughing away to himself. He had a plywood false bottom in the bucket and only the top 4 inches was mussels. He got the biggest charge out of it and we both laughed and laughed. His wife was in the car shaking her head, and said something to the effect of "and I got to live with him." I still think to myself that they must live a life of laughter.

Here is an excerpt from Ernest's email:

The only one that steals my mussels is my brother. I'll keep a watch for him (lol).

Incidentally, I've had a long association with mussels.

As near as I can remember, it started just after I gave up breast feeding in 1947 (lol).

I harvest mussels during any month having the letter "r" (i.e., from fall to spring).

I usually store them submerged off the wharf prior to cooking (for cleaning reasons).

I avoid removing their beards prior to cooking (to avoid damage or killing).

I add little or no water to a pot when cooking.

A mussel requires 2 to 3 years to grow, so I continually seed my bed with spats [very young mussels] from a floating dock. **LM**

On Cooking and Cleaning Mussels

We all have our own way to cook and clean mussels; we disagree on this as much we do about the best way to cook lobsters. Here's my say:

Empty the mussels into the sink right away after bringing them home, and do not insert the plug. Run cold water over the mussels and stir them around and around with your hands, then turn off the water. Go through the mussels one by one. If one is closed tight, it goes in the "good to cook" pile. If it's open, give it a knock against the side of the sink: it should close up tight—then it is good to cook. If the mussel doesn't close, throw it out.

The good mussels can be stored in a bowl covered with a damp cloth in the refrigerator for a day or so. Rinse again before cooking and make sure that none have opened. As you probably won't know for sure when they were harvested, you can't be sure how long they will last. Cook as soon as possible.

This recipe is for cooking 1 pound of mussels and can easily be scaled up.

Use a saucepan or pot with a cover that will give the mussels space to expand by one-third—you don't want to cram the mussels into the pot. Into the saucepan put 1 cup water, 2 tablespoons salt, a few slices of onion, ½ teaspoon peppercorns, a bay leaf, and a glug of beer or white wine. Bring to a boil and add the mussels. Cover. Let the water return to a boil and leave the mussels in just until they open wide. This usually takes about 5 minutes. After 5 minutes, remove the cover, and give the mussels a stir. If they are open, they are done; if not, give them a few more minutes.

Mussels are best steamed, not boiled; if you do have a steamer, use that and steam just until they open. **LM**

DRUNKEN MUSSELS

2 lb wild mussels (or 5 lb cultivated mussels)

2 tbsp butter

¼ cup onion, diced

2 cloves garlic, minced

1 bottle Quidi Vidi Iceberg beer

½ cup whipping cream (35% milk fat)

½ tsp lovage puree, optional

Salt and pepper

A loaf of crusty bread to sop up the liquid

Put a frying pan on low-medium heat. Melt the butter and fry the onions and garlic just until the onions are translucent. Add the beer and reduce the amount of liquid by half. Add the cream and reduce a little, to the desired consistency. Add the lovage purée. Season to taste and spread all over the mussels. Grab your favourite beer and enjoy! **LM**

STEAMED COD with CURRIED MUSSELS

In every culture there seems to be a holy trinity of vegetables. In some American recipes, especially Cajun cuisine, the mirepoix is peppers, onion, and celery. In Italian, Portuguese, and Spanish cuisine, it is onion, garlic, and tomato. Another common combination is onion, carrots, and celery. I like the Newfoundland trio of carrot, parsnip, and turnip. These are the root vegetables that tended to be in every root cellar right next to the coveted dry blue potatoes.

1 to 2 lb cod fillets, skinned and cut into portion sizes

½ lb mussels, cleaned and debearded (see page 198)

4 tbsp unsalted butter

1 small onion, thinly sliced

2 carrots, peeled and julienned

2 parsnips, peeled and julienned

1 small turnip, peeled and julienned

1 garlic clove, crushed

2 tsp mild curry powder

½ cup white wine

1 cup whipping cream

1 tbsp fresh coriander, chopped

Salt and pepper

Sprinkle salt over the cod portions and set aside for at least 20 minutes to allow the flesh to firm up. Place a large saucepan over medium heat and add the butter. Once the butter is melted, add the vegetables, garlic, and curry powder. Cover and sweat the vegetables for 5 minutes, until they are just beginning to soften.

Place a separate saucepan over a high heat. When it is hot, add the mussels, discarding any that are open or cracked. Add the wine. Cover and cook for 2 minutes or until all the mussels have opened.

Strain the mussels through a fine sieve, reserving the liquid. Add this liquid to the vegetables (be sure to leave behind any grit or sediment). Reduce the liquid in the vegetables by half over high heat, add the cream, and reduce to a consistency that thinly coats the vegetables. Pick the mussels from their shells and add to the vegetables and sauce. Keep warm.

Set a steamer over a saucepan of simmering water large enough to hold the cod pieces. Steam the cod for 6 to 10 minutes until it is cooked through.

To serve, spoon some of the vegetables and sauce into a bowl, sprinkle with fresh coriander, and place a piece of cod on top. Freshly grind some black pepper on top of the fish. Serve immediately. **MT**

CORNED COD

Like many a Newfoundland woman would say when you asked for a recipe for an old family favourite dish, "it's not much of a recipe really."

This is not much of a recipe, but I'll share with you how you can make easy salt fish—corned fish. Then wherever you are in the world, you can always make fish cakes like we do here at home.

If you don't already know, when someone says fish in Newfoundland, they mean cod. For this recipe, you can use cod, pollock, haddock, or any other white fish, even freshwater white fish. The flesh should be ¾ to 1 inch thick.

Use fine salt, not coarse or rock salt. This is very important; 10 to 15 hours is not long enough to dissolve rock salt and create an even distribution of salt.

For a piece of fish the length of your hand (about 7 inches), use 1 tablespoon of salt. That's a good heavy sprinkle on both sides of the fish. Dad liked his salted for just 3 hours, but he was just going to boil it and have it with boiled potatoes on the side (he would eat this three times a week, for sure). I prefer to leave my cod overnight in the refrigerator. About 10 to15 hours after it's been in the salt, I pat it dry, vacuum-seal it, and put it in the freezer.

This salt fish is perfect for fish cakes or to use for our Cod Boudain Blanc (page 131).

MILK POACHED SMOKED HALIBUT

1 smoked halibut steak
(or any smoked white fish)

2 tbsp butter, salted

2 shallots, thinly sliced

4 cloves garlic, thinly sliced

6 to 8 branches woody herb
(sweet gale, thyme, sage,
rosemary, oregano)

1 tsp all-purpose flour

4 cups whole milk, plus
more as needed

Zest of 1 lemon

2 tsp sea salt

½ tsp pepper, freshly ground

Pinch nutmeg

Melt the butter in a wide-bottomed frying pan over medium-high heat. Cook until the butter is brown and has a nutty aroma. Add the shallots and garlic and sauté for 3 to 4 minutes until golden. Scatter the herbs and flour into the pan. Cook, stirring often, for 1 minute. Gradually whisk in the milk and bring the mixture to a simmer. Add the lemon zest, salt, pepper, and nutmeg. Add the halibut to the pan and more milk to cover if needed. Bring the milk to a light simmer.

Cook until the halibut is heated through, approximately 5 minutes. Remove the halibut from the pan and keep warm. The poaching liquid may be reduced to create a sauce, if desired, to serve with your favourite side, such as fresh pasta, mashed potato, or a cheesy polenta. **MT**

MOOSE ALLOUETTES

My dear friend Vanessa has helped me immeasurably in growing Cod Sounds (my company), right from the beginning. She is the person you call when you need a let's-get-'er-done attitude. She's helped me build wood huts, entertain a crowd from CNN, and arrange big Jiggs' dinners for guests, and she's taxied around my kids when I asked. She means the world to me.

When I asked her for this recipe, she wrote: *This is a family recipe from my father. Growing up, we considered these a delicacy, as we had them only on holidays or during family get-togethers when we convinced Dad to get out a moose roast from the deep freeze. We'd savour every crumb. To this day, I remember the dining room table covered in spices and slices of moose and rolling these darlings up with tender love and care. You can use any kind of bacon but thick-sliced needs a longer cooking time. I hope you enjoy them as much as we did. I can still taste them every time I close my eyes and think about them.* **LM**

1 lb moose roast, sliced thin like bacon

1 pkg bacon

¼ cup garlic, dehydrated or fresh minced

¼ cup onion, dehydrated or fresh finely minced

1 tbsp red pepper flakes

1 tsp black pepper

1 tsp sea salt

1 tsp savory

Toothpicks

Lay the bacon slices on a flat surface. Lay one slice of moose meat on each slice of bacon (it's fine if the moose isn't as long as the bacon strip).

Combine the garlic, onion, red pepper flakes, black pepper, and sea salt in a small bowl, and mix thoroughly. Sprinkle this mixture evenly over the moose meat.

Roll up the meat with the spices so that the spices are on the inside and the bacon is on the outside. Keep each one together with a toothpick. Lay on a baking sheet. Sprinkle each alouette with a touch of savory. Bake at 375°F for 45 to 55 minutes until the bacon is crispy.

Recipe by Vanessa Kenny

Brining moose heart.

MOOSE HEART JERKY

In this recipe, I suggest smoking the heart for extra depth of flavour before making the jerky. The finished jerky can be stored in airtight containers for the perfect jerky on your next outdoor excursion.

1 moose heart, approximately 3 to 5 lb

PICKLING SPICE MIX

2 tbsp whole mustard seeds

2 tsp whole caraway seeds

1 tsp red pepper flakes

6 whole cloves

1 tsp ground allspice

1 tsp ground ginger

2 bay leaves, crumbled

2 cinnamon sticks, broken in half

2 tbsp dried sweet gale (or bay leaf)

1 tbsp black peppercorns

6 juniper berries

Combine pickling spice mix ingredients. Place in a jar with a tight lid. This will keep for up to a year.

Trim all visible fat and hard valve tissue from the moose heart. Rinse thoroughly. Bring 1 litre of water to a boil with the salt, pepper, bay leaves, juniper berries, pickling spice, and Prague powder. Make sure that all salts are dissolved. Let cool completely, then pour into a large nonreactive container. Add an additional 4 litres cold water. Refrigerate until fully chilled. This may take several hours. Of course, if you are making this in cold weather season, just put it outside until chilled.

Once the liquid is completely chilled, add the moose heart and weight it down to completely submerge it in the liquid. Place the filled container in the refrigerator or outside in a shed, if it is cold enough, for 7 days. Turn the heart about halfway through the curing time to redistribute the cure around all sides of the meat for even curing.

BRINE

1 lb 5 oz (600 g) salt, non-iodized or sea salt

1 oz (30 g) Prague powder #1

20 cups (5 litres) water

1 onion, chopped in quarters

2 tbsp pickling spice

1 cup brown sugar

Remove the heart from the brine, rinse, and pat dry. Place in a cold smoker for 2 hours. Remove and thinly slice.

To make the jerky, place the heart slices in a dehydrator set to the meat temperature setting and dry. **MT**

MOOSE TONGUE WITH RAISIN SAUCE

The tongue is another underutilized piece of game meat. To me, it is no different than any other muscle on a moose—just a slightly different texture, like that of the moose heart. It has a wonderful mild taste and pairs well with this sweet and savory sauce.

1 moose tongue

1 tsp salt

1 onion, sliced

1 clove garlic, chopped

Few peppercorns

1 sprig thyme

¾ cup brown sugar

3 tbsp cornstarch

¼ cup apple cider
or white vinegar

½ cup golden raisins

1 lemon, thinly sliced

1 tbsp oil or bacon fat

Cover the tongue with water in a medium pot. Add the salt, onion, garlic, peppercorns, and thyme. Bring to a boil. Reduce to a simmer and cover the pot. Cook until the tongue is tender, about 3½ hours. Remove the tongue from the pot and reserve 1½ cups broth for the sauce. When cool enough to handle, peel the skin from the tongue and discard. Let the tongue cool completely.

To make the sauce, mix all the remaining ingredients in the top of a double boiler and cook until the raisins are plump, about 5 to 10 minutes. Stir occasionally.

Slice the cooked, cooled tongue in slices approximately ¼ inch thick. Serve with the warm sauce on a bed of polenta for a meal, or with crusty grilled bread for happy hour. MT

RABBIT MORTADELLA

The first fall after I met Lori, she asked if I knew anyone who hunted rabbit with snares. She needed some to teach a rabbit butchery class. When I asked her how many she needed, I was a little unprepared to hear that she wanted 20 ... but she would take as many as she could get. I called my father on the west coast, who knew someone who could probably get that number on short notice before the season closed. He came through, and 24 rabbits were trucked across the island in time for the course.

Unfortunately, the course had to be cancelled, and we were stuck with 24 rabbits. We decided to split them between us. But what to do with 12 rabbits "with their jackets on" in my freezer? Rabbit meat can be gamey. The two most common rabbit preparations in Newfoundland are bottled rabbit (for later use) or rabbit pie. I was on the hunt for something different. I had been playing around with curing meats, so I decided to try rabbit. If you can make moose bologna, why not rabbit mortadella?

---

1 lb rabbit meat, medium grind

1 tsp garlic powder

2 tbsp white wine

1 tbsp salt

½ tsp Prague powder #1

½ dried apricots, cut in quarters

½ cup gin or other spirit, optional

Mix the rabbit meat, garlic, white wine, salt, and Prague powder together well. Place in the freezer for about ½ hour. While the meat is cooling, soak the chopped apricots in your choice of spirit (the spirit is not necessary, but it adds a nice flavour).

In a food processor or countertop blender, combine the meat mixture, crushed ice, alder bud powder, nutmeg, coriander, and sweet gale until the mixture is whipped. Scoop this mixture into a bowl and fold in the pork fat and nuts. Drain the apricots and add.

1 lb crushed ice

1 tsp winter alder buds,
toasted and finely ground

½ tsp nutmeg

1 tsp ground coriander

¼ tsp ground dried sweet gale

½ cup walnuts

½ cup pork fat,
cut in ½-inch cubes

Spray a ham-maker cylinder with nonstick spray and fill it with the meat mixture, making sure that it is packed tightly, with no air pockets. Poach the meat mixture in a water bath up to the level of the meat in the container until the internal temperature reaches 170°F. If you do not have a ham maker, poach the meat mixture in any tall heatproof dish or bread pan. You can also make a tube with multiple layers of plastic wrap tied off tightly at both ends.

Cool the mortadella completely in the refrigerator before taking it out of the mould. Slice thinly for sandwiches or for your next charcuterie board. **MT**

50¢ a Rabbit

I remember Mom describing how people would, at one time, sell rabbits along the highway in the fall of the year. And the younger boys that didn't yet drive would often go door to door selling them: 50 cents a rabbit. My brother telling me that he would check his slips before he went to school.

You would most often see rabbits for sale up on the highway at the crossroads—it's the best spot to catch people going by and those going down to the communities along the shore. The car bonnets would be lined with rabbits, according to my mother. Nan says that in her time the men would go off "gunnin" (shooting rabbits) for the day, bring them home, and "that was it, they never had nothing more to do with them." It was then that the women's work started. The rabbits would be tied up in the old shed (6 or 8 or more at a time) and then taken down and cleaned as they wanted them for supper. It was the fall and winter when they hunted, so the rabbits were kept cold and often froze. The women did the skinning, the gutting, and the cooking. Safe to say the cleaning up, too.

While we in Newfoundland usually refer to these animals as rabbits, they are more often snowshoe hare.

Rabbit Risotto
with Rabbit Roulade.

When I worked in restaurants in St. John's, the rice for risotto was always precooked. You can certainly do this a day or two ahead, or earlier in the day, and finish it for supper. Just pull the rice off the heat when you are about halfway through adding the stock, let it cool, and place in the fridge. When you are ready to finish it off, bring the stock back to a simmer, bring the pan holding the rice back up to heat, and pick up where you left off.

RABBIT RISOTTO

The rabbit can be prepared days ahead of making this dish. After roasting, remove the meat and keep it in the fridge for up to 5 days. I also vacuum-pack and freeze portions of cooked rabbit meat, which makes it easy to grab a pack for a quick last-minute supper of pasta, ravioli, or this risotto dish. Who ever thought that you would say that about rabbit?

PULLED RABBIT

1 whole rabbit, cut in pieces (remove the legs from the hip; remove the back just below the ribcage; and leave the front legs attached to the rib, so you have just four pieces, as this will help with removing the meat from the bones later)

1 onion, chopped

2 cloves garlic, chopped

¼ cup celery, chopped

1 bay leaf

1 cup red wine

1 cup game stock

½ tsp salt

½ tsp pepper

Prepare the rabbit

Preheat the oven to 350°F. Place a Dutch oven with a tight-fitting lid on a medium heat. Add the butter and oil. Sear the rabbit on all sides. Sprinkle with ½ tsp each of salt and pepper. Add the onions, garlic, celery, bay leaf, wine, and stock. Cover tightly with aluminum foil and the lid and place it in the oven. After 1½ hours, check on the rabbit. If the meat falls easily away from the bone, it's done. If not, give it another 30 minutes. Remove from the oven and let it cool. Remove the leg, back, and front quarter meat. Pay attention around the ends of the legs as you remove the meat. Rabbit bones splinter easily—they are sharp, hard bones—and you don't want to bite down on a piece of bone and crack yourself a tooth or a denture.

RISOTTO

2 cups arborio rice

4 cups game stock
(or other stock)

2 tbsp salted butter

2 tbsp olive oil

¼ cup diced onion

1 clove garlic, minced

1 cup fresh Parmesan, grated
with a micro plane or finest
side on a box grater

½ cup dehydrated winter
chanterelle mushrooms
(or fresh mushrooms)

Make the risotto

Bring the stock to a simmer in a small saucepan. Add the butter and olive oil to a larger saucepan on medium or medium-low heat. Add the rice and stir until you have slightly golden rice. Add the onions, garlic, and mushrooms. Right away, start adding the stock, one ladleful at a time, stirring while it absorbs the liquid. As soon as the stock is absorbed, add another ladleful and stir. Continue until the rice is creamy but still has a slight bite. This should take 20 to 30 minutes. You may not use all the stock—but if you run out, have the kettle boiled and use water.

When the rice is ready, add the Parmesan cheese and pulled rabbit meat and serve right away. The risotto should be loose but not pool liquid as you plate it. The risotto in the pot will very quickly dry up, so keep a kettle close by and add a little boiling water if needed before you serve it. **LM**

Two-Toned Chanterelle Ravioli.

TWO-TONED CHANTERELLE RAVIOLI

This recipe uses a mixer with a pasta roller attachment. The dough can also be made by hand and fed through a counter-mounted pasta roller.

NETTLE EGG PASTA

4 large eggs

3½ cups sifted
all-purpose flour

½ teaspoon sea salt

2 cups fresh nettle leaves, packed

SEMOLINA EGG PASTA

4 large eggs

1 tbsp olive oil

3⅓ cups semolina flour

½ tsp sea salt

You will be making 2 separate batches of dough for this recipe.

Place the flour for the nettle pasta in a blender with the nettle leaves. Blend on high to finely grind the leaves into the flour. I find that this works better than using blanched chopped leaves for better control of the amount of moisture in the pasta dough.

For both pastas, place all ingredients except the flour in the bowl and quickly mix with the regular mixer paddle. Add all the flour and roughly mix for about 30 seconds. Remove the paddle and replace with the dough hook. While the machine is on, gradually and slowly add enough water until the dough comes together as a ball and is not sticky. Continue kneading for 3 to 5 minutes. Remove the dough from the mixer, knead by hand into a smooth ball, cover, and place on the counter to rest for at least 20 minutes.

While the dough rests, make the filling by thoroughly mixing all filling ingredients in a bowl. Set aside. Divide each type of dough into 4 pieces and process one piece of each with a pasta roller. Start with the widest setting, reducing by one number at a time until your pasta is one away from the thinnest setting on your pasta roller. If you roll to the thinnest setting, the pasta may not hold in the filling when you cook it. You will now have one green and one yellow sheet of pasta. Keep a pastry brush and a small bowl of room

RICOTTA CHANTERELLE FILLING

26 oz fresh ricotta cheese

1 cup chanterelles, finely chopped, sautéed in unsalted butter

1 cup grated Parmesan cheese

¼ tsp pepper, freshly ground

½ tsp nettle seeds

temperature water nearby to seal the dough. Lay one dough sheet out on a large, flat surface lightly dusted with flour. Semolina flour is ideal, since it won't make your dough gummy if it gets moistened, but all-purpose flour is perfectly fine. Cut each sheet in half. You should have two pieces of dough roughly 15 inches long and 5 inches wide; each makes approximately 12 ravioli. Cover the other two halves with a towel to keep from drying out.

Moisten the dough lightly with the water using a pastry brush. Place 12 tablespoons of filling evenly across one sheet of dough in two rows of six. Place the other sheet of pasta on top of the filled pasta sheet, pressing from the centre outward to remove the excess air. Watch out for air bubbles, but also accept that a little air is inevitable. Be sure to press out as much air as you can. Gently pat the dough down around each lump of filling to create a seal. Finally, use the fluted side of a ravioli cutter or a stamp to slice the ravioli into even squares. A knife will do in a pinch.

Toss the ravioli into a pot of salted water at a low boil, and cook for approximately 3 minutes, or until slicing into one piece reveals no starchy line in the centre.

Serve the ravioli in the sauce of your choice—for me, a great filling requires little more than a drizzle of olive oil and perhaps some chopped herbs or a sage brown butter sauce. Finish with a dusting of freshly grated Parmesan. **MT**

VANESSA'S BLUEBERRY DUFF

This was always a staple with our Jiggs' dinners. We would throw it right on top of all the meat and vegetables and cover it with gravy, leave it plain, or use a little rum sauce. It was never dessert, but just a part of the dinner and like every other part of a Jiggs' dinner for me—and if you were missing one part, you may as well be missing them all.

2½ cups all-purpose flour

¾ cup white sugar

2 tsp baking powder

1 to 1½ cups frozen or fresh blueberries

⅓ cup melted butter

¾ cup 2% or whole milk

1 tsp vanilla

RUM SAUCE (OPTIONAL)

6 tbsp unsalted butter

¾ cup brown sugar

⅓ cup whipping cream

3 tbsp dark rum

Splash of vanilla

Mix together the flour, sugar, and baking powder. Add the blueberries and toss them in the dry mixture. Pour in the melted butter, milk, and vanilla. Mix together until no lumps remain.

Pour the batter into a pudding steamer or pudding bag. If using a pudding bag, tie it together at the top with string and attach it to the side of the pot. Don't allow it to touch the bottom of the pot or it will stick. Alternatively, lay the pudding steamer in water in the pot.

Steam for 1½ to 2 hours. Remove the duff from the bag or steamer, slice, and serve.

To make the rum sauce, melt the butter in a small saucepan, add the brown sugar, and stir until the sugar is dissolved. Whisk in the rum, vanilla, and cream. Let it cool or serve warm (the sauce will get thicker as it cools). Pour over the duff.

Recipe by Vanessa Kenny

LORI'S GREAT-GRANDMOTHER'S GINGERBREAD

Crosby's molasses was a staple in our family as it was in many homes in Newfoundland. It really does speak to long-standing traditions, cookies, cakes, and Christmas. My children's grandmother, Regina McCarthy, bakes amazing, perfectly crisp, gingersnap cookies every year. They always come in a Christmas tin that we return every year, and she refills it the next. It's the only time of year they are made and are one of our favourite treats of the Christmas season.

Ginger cakes, however, show up year-round and I do believe this is the oldest recipe from my mom's family. While it may have come on the back of the Crosby's molasses container at one point (like so many other "family" recipes), we have, for as long as I can remember, called it great-grandmother's gingerbread. We do love a romantic story of food here in Newfoundland, and if there isn't one, we've been known to make one up. In the end, it matters not where the recipe came from, but only that it has brought a lifetime of memories to cherish—from coming home as a child to the house smelling of gingerbread cake, to serving it on the beach to guests and sending them off with the recipe.

This makes a quick last-minute dessert and is best cooked in a well-greased and floured tube pan. **LM**

½ cup white sugar

½ cup shortening

1½ tsp baking soda

1 tsp cinnamon

1 tsp ginger

1 egg

1 cup molasses

2½ cups all-purpose flour

½ tsp cloves

½ tsp salt

1 cup hot water

Preheat the oven to 350°F. Mix the cinnamon, ginger, cloves, baking soda, and salt in a small bowl. Melt the shortening and put it in a large mixing bowl. Stir the brown sugar into the melted shortening and then add the molasses and egg. Beat well. Add the dry ingredients and hot water alternately. Pour into a well-greased and floured tube pan and bake for 30 to 40 minutes. Test with a long skewer to make sure that the middle is cooked.

Don't forget the love.

Recipe by Alfreda Baker

The Cake

My husband and I took a quick vacation to New York one year before Christmas and stayed at the famous Waldorf Astoria Hotel in Manhattan. We made sure to make a reservation at the restaurant in the hotel, the Bull and Bear. We were sure to order one item from the menu that night: the famous carrot cake.

Famous, because I had been entrusted with a sacred family recipe passed down to only the girls in the Tulk family. On the recipe card my mother-in-law had written:

> *Gran Tulk kept this recipe within the family circle. The story behind it—Gran's sister Madge in Halifax and her friend visited New York and had lunch at the Waldorf Astoria. This cake was served, and the friend asked the chef for his recipe of the cake. He obliged her with his recipe and a bill for $250! Gran always called this "The Cake."*

I wasn't sure if I would receive a copy, since I was only married into the clan, not born into it. I have made this recipe for my husband's birthday for many years. When we received the menu at the Bull and Bear and scanned the dessert selection, we were surprised not to see carrot cake listed at all. Under the B&B Bread Pudding and, of course, New York Cheesecake was the Waldorf Astoria Original Red Velvet Cake. We placed our order and asked about the carrot cake. The waiter politely said that he had never seen a carrot cake on the menu in the many years that he had worked there. We ordered, received, and thoroughly enjoyed our meal, ending it with Red Velvet Cake and an aperitif.

We never questioned the authenticity of the recipe story until recently. Apparently, it is a common story that many families have told: the sacred carrot cake recipe being passed on through generations. If you search the web, hundreds of personal posts will come up about this cake. I will still make it for my husband each March for his birthday with some beautiful sweet carrots from Butler's farm in Holyrood from my root cellar. It will be even better than the last. **MT**

tsp. salt
tsp. baking soda
tsp baking powder
grated carrot
sliced brazil nuts
cinnamon
above mixture and beat until
blended. Add in carrot and
nuts. Pour in pans.
Baking time 1 hour.

THE WALDORF ASTORIA CARROT CAKE

CAKE

1 cup white sugar

1 cup vegetable oil

3 large eggs

1⅓ cups all-purpose flour

½ tsp salt

1⅓ tsp baking powder

1⅓ tsp baking soda

1⅓ tsp cinnamon

2 cups carrots, finely grated

1 cup slivered Brazil nuts
or walnuts

FROSTING

8 oz cream cheese

2 cups icing sugar

¼ cup butter

2 tsp vanilla

Preheat the oven to 300°F and grease two 8-inch round cake pans.

Combine the sugar and vegetable oil and beat well. Add the eggs one at a time, beating well between each addition. Sift together the flour, baking soda, baking powder, and cinnamon. Add to the egg mixture and beat well. Fold in the grated carrots and nuts. Pour into the pans. Bake for 1 hour. Cool completely.

Mix all ingredients for the frosting until completely smooth.

Place one cooled cake on a cake plate. Cover with one-third of the frosting mixture. Place the other cake on top of the iced cake. Use the rest of the icing on the final cake. Decorate with candied carrot swirls and crushed nuts.

Recipe by Madeline Tulk

The Long and Hungry Month of March

In Newfoundland and Labrador, the month of March has traditionally been referred to as "the long and hungry month of March." The expression finds its origins in our food history.

The "long" is taken from the fact that March follows the shortest month in the year, February. The "hungry month" can be explained by looking at the availability of food, especially root vegetables and how supplies were preserved throughout the winter months.

The coming of March marked a time of optimism and hope. March was the "swilin' time," or seal hunting season. Seal meat would give some reprieve in the long and hungry month of March, by which time the family food store was very low. At this time of the year, in many parts of the province, sealing provided the only opportunity to obtain fresh meat and the pelts brought long-awaited cash.

It would be springtime before the hope of the first new vegetable of the year would show, the spring green, know locally as dandelion leaves, the first vegetable after a long winter.

Larry Dohey,
archivalmoments.ca

What Is a Root Cellar?

The preservation of food for our ancestors (before the weekly and for some daily visit to the grocery or convenience store) typically involved freezing, salting, or pickling.

With no electricity, one of the essential structures to be built on the family property was the "root cellar." Root cellars served to keep food supplies from freezing during the winter months and cool during the summer months.

Typically, families would put a variety of root vegetables in the cellar in the fall of the year; the main vegetables being potatoes, turnip, and carrot. Other food supplies placed in the root cellar over the winter months included beets, preserves, jams, berries, and pickled cabbage. Fish and wild game also found a place in the cellars including turres, moose, caribou, salt meat, and salt fish. In addition to what was stored in the cellar, some families had access to domestic animals such as cows, goats, and sheep.

Larry Dohey,
archivalmoments.ca

WILD BERRY CHEESECAKE

I love cheesecake but I needed an easy recipe. This one hasn't failed me yet. Feel free to substitute whatever berry you have in your freezer. I've tried them all. Did I mention I really like cheesecake?

1¾ cups crushed Purity gingersnaps

2 tbsp salted butter, melted

1 cup white sugar, divided

8 oz cream cheese

1 cup Greek yogurt

1 tsp vanilla

3 eggs, room temperature

TOPPING

3 cups fresh or frozen berries

¼ cup water

3 tbsp sugar

1 tbsp lemon juice

1 cup extra berries for garnish

Preheat the oven to 350°F and grease a 9-inch springform pan. Combine the crushed gingersnaps, butter, and ¼ cup sugar. Pour this mixture into the pan and press firmly to make a crust. Bake the crust for 10 minutes and then let cool. Reduce the oven to 325°F.

When the crust reaches room temperature, wrap the outside of the pan with two layers of aluminum foil, making sure there are no gaps that would allow water to seep in. Place the springform pan into a larger pan. Boil the kettle and set aside.

With a handheld mixer, beat the cream cheese until smooth. Add the remaining sugar and beat for a minute at medium speed. Add the yogurt and vanilla and mix well. Scrape down the bowl with a spatula when needed. Add the eggs one at a time and mix on low speed after each addition until blended well. Pour the batter onto the crust.

Place the double pans in the oven and pour the boiling water into the larger pan to make a water bath. The water level should be about 1 inch up the side of the inner pan. Bake for about 1½ hours until the centre of the cheesecake is almost set. Turn off the oven, leave the oven door ajar and let the cheesecake sit for another hour.

Meanwhile, prepare the topping. Combine the berries, sugar, and ¼ cup water in a saucepan and bring to a boil. Boil it until it thickens. Add the lemon juice and simmer for 1 to 2 minutes. Let cool.

Remove the cheesecake from the oven and remove it from the water bath. Let it cool to room temperature. Remove the springform pan rim and top the cheesecake with the berry topping. Garnish with the extra berries and chill the cheesecake for at least 4 hours before serving. **MT**

Basic Homespun Vamps

I have always been a crafter. I'm not a reader but I need something to do in those rare bits of free time, like driving across the island. I have tried most traditional crafting techniques—crocheting, quilting, sewing, and knitting. My mother taught me how to knit as her father had taught her. I love making vamps because it is a quick project: easy to put down and pick up later. Plus, everyone loves a pair of double-knit vamps.

FOOT SIZES	
SMALL	7½ to 9 inches / 19 to 23 cm
MEDIUM	9 to 10½ inches / 23 to 27 cm
LARGE	10½ to 12 inches / 27 to 31 cm

The basic pattern for these vamps is from a knitting booklet from Memorial University of Newfoundland. It has been reprinted, but my version, which belonged to my grandmother, is from 1980. It was an initiative of the Division of Adult and Continuing Education Department of MUN and Anna Templeton, who, at the time, was the supervisor of Craft Training. Templeton collaborated with knitting groups from across the island on the booklet "Operation Homespun." Designed as a helpful guide to all who were interested in knitting and to document traditional patterns and designs used in Newfoundland, the booklet encouraged the use of pure homespun wool. Emphasizing the fundamentals of knitting, it contained tips and patterns for socks, mitts, and sweaters for every family member, plus ski sweaters and double-knit trigger mitts. My copy is well worn and much loved. I hope you enjoy my version of the homespun vamp. It is my go-to gift for both family and friends. **MT**

The instructions are written for size small (S) with changes for medium (M) and large (L) in parentheses S (M, L). If you wish, you can use one colour for the whole pattern—you do not have to integrate a pattern into the top and sole. Or you can use two colours, one for the main part and one for the pattern and sole. You can also use three colours, as in the photograph. It's a great way to use up partial balls of wool leftover from other knitting projects. You can start and stop the colours wherever you wish, but the easiest places are before and after shaping the heel and before shaping the toe.

MATERIALS:
Small = 1 skein
Medium = 1 skein
Large = 2 skeins
1 set size 8 (4.00) double pointed needles

TENSION:
10 stitches and 13 rows =
2 inches or 5 cm on size 8 (4.00) needles

SOCK INSTRUCTIONS:
Cast on 36 (44, 48) stitches and space on three needles S-12, 12, 12 (M-14, 16, 14) (L-16, 16, 16). Work for 18 rounds. The top will start to curl (perfect to roll over Blundstones). If you prefer a longer length, add more rounds to the ankle.

TO ARRANGE HEEL STITCHES:
Slip 2 (3, 3) stitches from end of the 1st needle onto the beginning of the 2nd needle and 2 (3, 3) stitches from the beginning of the 3rd needle onto the end of the 2nd needle. 10, 16, 10 (11, 22, 11) (13, 22, 13) for instep. Divide the 16 (22, 22) stitches on the 2nd needle onto 2 needles and leave for the instep. Knit the stitches of the 1st needle onto the end of the 3rd needle.

Working on these 20 (22, 26) stitches, proceed:

Next row: K1, P8 (P9, P11), P2 together, P8 (P9, P11), K1. There are now 19 (21, 25) stitches on the needle.

TO MAKE HEEL:

1st row: *K1, Sl1 (being careful not to tighten the yarn behind the slipped stitch). Repeat from * to the last stitch. K1.

2nd row: K1, Purl to the last stitch. K1. Repeat these 2 rows 7 (8, 9) times more, then the 1st row once.

TO SHAPE HEEL:

1st row: P10 (10, 12), P2 together, P1. Turn.
2nd row: K3, Sl1, K1, pass over, K1. Turn.
3rd row: P4, P2 together, P1. Turn.
4th row: K5, Sl1, K1, pass over, K1. Turn.
5th row: P6, P2 together, P1. Turn.
6th row: K7, Sl1, K1, pass over, K1. Turn.
7th row: P8, P2 together, P1. Turn.
8th row: K9, Sl1, K1, pass over, K1. Turn. (11 stitches on the needle for S)

M size only:

9th row: P10, P2 together, P1. Turn.
10th row: K10, Sl1, K1, pass over. (11 stitches on the needle for M)

L size only:

9th row: P10, P2 together, P1. Turn.
10th row: K11, Sl1, K1, pass over, K1. Turn.
11th row: P12, P2 together, P1. Turn.
12th row: K12, Sl1, K1, pass over. Turn. (13 stitches on the needle for L)

TO MAKE INSTEP:

Put the 16 (22, 22) stitches for the instep on one needle.

1st needle: With the right side of the work facing and using the needle with 11 (11, 13) heel stitches, pick up and knit 9 (10, 11) stitches, inserting the needle through the knot formed by the knitted stitch, at the beginning and end of each row.

2nd needle: Knit across 16 (22, 22) stitches for the instep.

3rd needle: Pick up and knit 9 (10, 11) stitches along the other side of heel, then knit 5 (5, 6) stitches from the 1st needle.

Stitches are now divided as follows:

1st needle: 15 (16, 18)
2nd needle: 16 (22, 22)
3rd needle: 14 (15, 17)

* At this point, if you are integrating an image on the top of the foot, start your second colour here and alternate colours on the sole (see graph).

Proceed:

1st round: Knit.
2nd round:
   1st needle: Knit to the last 3 stitches. K2 together. K1.
   2nd needle: Knit.
   3rd needle: K1, Sl1, K1, pass over. Knit to the end of the needle.

Repeat these 2 rounds until 8 (11, 11) stitches remain on the 1st needle, 16 (22, 22) on the 2nd needle, and 7 (10, 10) on the 3rd needle. 31 (43, 43) stitches on the round.

* At this point, if you are knitting an image on the top of the foot, start the image pattern with the second colour on the needle with 22 stitches. Don't forget that the pattern is 20 stitches wide and there

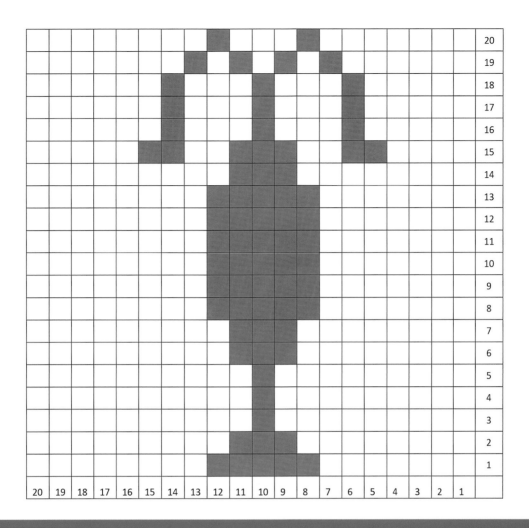

Anna Catherine Templeton was born in St. John's, the second eldest in the business family of R.A. Templeton. She was educated at Prince of Wales College and earned a pre-science degree at Memorial College before studying Home Economics at MacDonald College in Montreal. In 1938, Anna returned home to become a Field Worker, then Organizing Secretary of the Jubilee Guilds of Newfoundland and Labrador. With this job, she began a lifelong involvement with craft development and women's work in the province. She traveled the province alone, teaching other women, an unusual task for an urban, single, young woman of the upper middle class in the 1930s and 1940s. Her exceptional contribution to craft education provided the foundation for contemporary efforts in craft development. In 1994, the new Textile Studies Centre of the College of the North Atlantic was named the Anna Templeton Centre in her honour. It continues the tradition of innovation and creativity so loved by Anna Templeton.

From **Women's Walk: A Women's History Walk through Old St. John's,** *a booklet by the Women's History Group, 1997*

are 22 stitches on this needle, so start the pattern on the 2nd stitch. Continue the pattern on the sole as well.

Continue in plain knitting until the work (from where the stitches were picked up for the instep) measures 4 inches (5, 6 inches) or the desired length (10, 12.5, 15 cm).

Knit one round, decreasing 1 stitch on the 2nd needle.

TO SHAPE TOE:
1st round:

   1st needle: Knit to the last 3 stitches. K2 together, K1.

   2nd needle: K1, Sl1, K1, pass over. Knit to the last 3 stitches. K2 together, K1.

   3rd needle: K1, Sl1, K1, pass over. Knit to the end of the needle.

2nd round:

   Knit across each needle.

Repeat these 2 rounds to 10 (14, 14) stitches in the round. Knit the stitches of the 1st needle onto the end of the 3rd needle.

Break the yarn, leaving an end about 12 inches (30 cm) long, and graft the toe as instructed.

TO GRAFT THE TOE:
Thread a blunt ended needle with the yarn left at the toe. The needle from which the yarn hangs should be at the back.

* Insert the needle as for a knit stitch into the 1st stitch on the front needle and slip it off the needle. Then insert the needle as for a purl stitch into the 2nd stitch on the front knitting needle and let it remain on the needle; pull the yarn through both of these stitches. Taking the yarn under the front knitting needle, now work on the back needle: holding the sewing needle for both of the following actions, insert the sewing needle as for purling into the 1st stitch on the back needle and slip it off the needle, then insert the sewing needle as for a knit stitch into the 2nd stitch on the back needle and, letting it remain on the needle, pull the yarn through both of these stitches.

Bring the yarn forward under the knitting needles and repeat from * until all stitches have been worked off.

Take the yarn to the inside of the work and darn in.

To make thicker and larger socks in all 3 sizes, the same pattern can be followed but use 3 ply wool and No. 7 (4.50) needles.

wild-crafted pantry

Not everything we used in recipes in this book are included in this wild harvesting section. We decided to omit, for example, the best-known berries, including blueberries and wild strawberries.

This is not meant to be a complete guide to wild harvesting. By no means should you carry this book off into the woods with you and start picking and tasting—you may not come back out!

Throughout this book, we refer to plants by the common names we know and use; because there are often many common names for one plant, we provide the Latin (scientific) names. This will help you understand what the plant is when we refer to it and help with your own foraging adventures.

The harvesting seasons refer to those of the east coast of the island of Newfoundland, as that is where we do most of our harvesting.

Please, before you harvest, be absolutely sure that you know what you are picking and the sustainable practices for doing so. We want to make sure that we are helping these plants thrive and regenerate to be here for generations to enjoy. Take only what you need and can process, take less than one-third of the plant and less than one-third of the plants, as far as your eye can see of a particular species. Consider that these species play a role in the larger ecosystem and they are not there just for our consumption. Let these thoughts guide you as you pick.

Alder – *Alnus* sp.
Season: November–May

Male alder catkins have a peppery flavour. Toast catkins slowly in a frying pan or bake at 200°F until brittle but not darkened. Catkins can be ground and used to flavour brines or meats, just as you would use pepper.

Beach lovage – *Ligusticum scoticum*
Season: June–September

The young spring leaves make an excellent pesto, and throughout the summer the leaves are used to flavour soups and stews. You can use beach lovage leaves as you would parsley. The flowers can be added to salads, carpaccio, and butters. The seeds are edible and add a nice crunch to dishes. The dried seeds can be used as a spice, which has a licorice flavour similar to that of fennel.

Beach orache – *Atriplex cristata*
Season: July–September

Used primarily as a salad green or garnish. Young beach orache is the go-to salad beach green; it has a slightly salty flavour and a succulent texture akin to that of spinach. It is one of those plants that I use as a vegetable rather than as a spice or flavouring. It's best in July, but the seed heads a little later in the season can also be harvested and added to salads for a nice little pop in your mouth.

Beach peas – *Lathyrus japonicus*
Season: June–August
This plant is enjoyable for a short window of time, one completely based on the weather, which is quite unpredictable here. As the beach pea shoots emerge from the ground, and until they are about 4 to 6 inches long, they are at their most delicious. During the first growth, they can be used as a salad green. The flowers are delicious, but the peas are basically inedible.

Chaga – *Inonotus obliguus*
Season: Year-round
Tea is the most common use for this fungus; however, I have made kombucha and tinctures from it, all with great success. Chaga has gained popularity among the medicinal mushrooms as well. Do your research before buying and/or harvesting it. When plants and fungus reach "superfood" status, proper regenerative harvesting practices are often not followed.

Chanterelles – *Cantharellus* sp.
Season: August–October
Use this meaty delicious mushroom wherever you would use any mushroom. After harvesting and cleaning, sauté any chanterelles you're not using immediately in butter and freeze in muffin tins to enjoy them year-round. Pop them out when frozen by sitting the muffin tin in a shallow bath of hot water until the butter melts enough to get them out. Place in a zipper bag and freeze. Pull them out of the freezer to make risotto, omelettes, a mushroom butter sauce for steak, or any number of other uses.

Chickweed – *Stellaria media*
Season: June–August

Use chickweed in salads; it can be used in quantity. Chickweed is best picked in the vegetable garden (where it tends to show up among rows of vegetables) in the first two to three weeks after it has emerged. Flowers are also edible.

Crowberries – *Empetrum nigrum*
Season: August–October

Traditionally, Nan would put these in steamed puddings (as I have been told many times). Crowberries are not a sweet berry—they are quite dry actually—but, added to ripe raspberries or blueberries, they are a delicious childhood memory for sure. Their distinct smell is of the July woods, when the bushes start to grow and the berries are coming out. A lady in Labrador told me about using crowberry bushes to smoke Arctic char and salmon. I've tried it with salmon and it's lovely.

Dandelion – *Taraxacum officinale*
Season: May–September

Traditionally, the leaves were the only part of the dandelion that was eaten, and usually just the first growth. According to my mother, the leaves become bitter when the buds and flowers come out. Recently, we have made some beautiful discoveries: dandelion buds make a great pickle, and the fresh flowers are lovely in tea buns and ice cream. Dandelions are always a welcome sign after the long haul of winter.

Dulse – *Palmaria pamata*
Season: January–May
Most species of dulse grow from January to spring, and this is when they are at their most delicious. Dulse, a mild-flavoured seaweed, is plentiful along our shores. It makes a delicious smoked seaweed. Enjoy a day chasing tides, harvesting dulse, and picking periwinkles and limpets.

Fireweed – *Chamaenerion angustifolius*
Season: May–August
Fireweed is a perennial found in disturbed or farmed areas, roadsides, and near the ocean. The spring shoots are a delicious substitute for asparagus. Harvest fireweed shoots 6 to 8 inches tall to sauté, roast, or pickle. After flowering, the stalks are fibrous and bitter; the flowers and leaves are edible. Toss raw leaves into a salad. Use flowers for garnish, to make fireweed jelly, or dry them for tea.

Goose tongue – *Plantago maritima*
Season: May–August
May/June and early July are best for goose tongue's texture and flavour. Sauté goose tongue with a little olive oil or butter and enjoy as a side vegetable.

Gutweed – *Ulva intestinalis*
Season: May–August

As gutweed is most often found where fresh water runs into salt, pick from extremely clean waterways and as far from humans as possible. This is a species of sea lettuce, delicate and delicious when fresh. Dehydrated, it has a lovely green colour and a mild flavour: sprinkle atop any fish or vegetable dish.

Japanese knotweed – *Reynoutria japonica*
Season: April–May

A savage invasive plant, but absolutely delicious! One of the first shoots to forage in the spring, Japanese knotweed is picked when it is 2 to 3 inches above the ground. Its pink colour, asparagus-like texture, and lemony flavour are a lovely addition to many dishes. The window for picking is very short; one of my favourite ways to prepare it is by lacto-fermentation so that I can enjoy it all year.

Juniper berry – *Juniperus communis*
Season: Year-round

Traditionally used as you would bay leaf in wild game dishes, this is still the most common use of this "berry" today. Pick only the blue fruit and leave the green ones to ripen; dry on the counter or in a dehydrator. Once dried, store in a tight-lidded bottle for year-round use. I grind them with equal parts salt by weight and use on game meat. Do not consume this wild plant while pregnant.

Labrador tea – *Rhododendron groenlandicum*

Season: May–September

As with most plants, the new fresh green-ery of Labrador tea hosts the most flavour and aroma. To make tea, it is important to steep the leaves in water *after* it has been boiled; do not boil the leaves in the water as this releases a toxin (*andromedotoxin*). These leaves also make a wonderful addi-tion to mushroom broths.

Oyster plant – *Mertensia maritima*

Season: May–September

Oyster plants, with their blue-green hue, are a spectacular sight across the beach-es. Leaves are best in salads, and the flowers make a beautiful addition on any dish. Early growth leaves are best.

Pine – *Pinus* sp.

Season: Year-round

Harvest pine needles year-round for teas, salt, and sugar, but the first growth (pine tips) have a fresher flavour. Grind well and make pine salt or sugar, which can be added to fish dishes or, in small quan-tities, to desserts.

Rose – *Rosa* sp.
Season: July–December
Rose hips have a long tradition of being made into jams and jellies in Newfoundland. Today, I also collect the petals to grind with sugar for a scented baking addition. Rose petal sugar is used in tea buns, syrups, and cakes.

Sea sandwort – *Honckenya peploides*
Season: May–August
Best early in the season, the top 2 inches of this plant are ideal for a brined pickle. The leaves have a fresh cucumber-like flavour and can be added to salad. Later in the season, the little white flowers are lovely atop a salad.

Sorrel
– *Rumex acetosella / Rumex acetosa*
Season: May–July
Sorrel leaves give a delicious lemony/acidic bright kick to tartares and salads. Use also to make wild sorrel soups.

Spruce – *Picea mariana/glauca*
Season: June

Pick and enjoy spruce tips in late spring. Pop used spruce tips to make beer, once common practice. Use spruce tips as you would rosemary. Spruce tips covered with honey and left to sit in the sun for a few days make a delicious, flavoured honey.

Stinging nettle – *Urtica dioica*
Season: April–July

Steam nettle leaves as you would any green, and add to pasta, pesto, or gnocchi. They make a nice green tea as well. The young fresh leaves are best.

Stinging nettle seeds – *Urtica dioica*
Season: May–June

As with picking stinging nettle leaves, you will want to wear gloves when harvesting the seeds. The seeds appear 6 to 8 weeks after the plants have emerged. Snip the entirety of the seeds in a 6- to 8-inch piece of the plant. Dehydrate the seeds on 120F for 3 to 4 hours. Pull the seeds off the plant and store in a well-sealed glass jar for later use. The seeds have a fairly neutral flavour but they add a nice crunch to salads, porridge, or shakes.

Sweet gale – *Myricia gale*
Season: Year-round (leaves/buds)

Leaves bloom in June and are at their best for the first few months. I gather quite a lot of them and dry them for use throughout the year. Use the leaves as you would thyme, rosemary, or bay leaf. The female sweet gale buds have a sweet-smelling aroma and can be steeped as a tea. The buds are available for picking all winter long; I gather them for year-round use.

Wild caraway seeds – *Carum carvi*
Season: August – September

These seeds are such a delight to find! I often find them around meadows near the seashore and sometimes on the banks of fresh water rivers. The entirety of the seed head is harvested then dehydrated on 120F for 3to 4 hours. Store in a well-sealed glass jar for later use. They made a wonderful addition to bread.

Wintercress – *Barbarea vulgaris*
Season: May-July

A member of the mustard family, wintercress is a fantastic salad green before it flowers. The small yellow flowers can be used in salads, tartares, and other savoury dishes—but once the flowers are out, the leaves are more bitter than pleasant. Wintercress leaves make an excellent lacto-ferment when roughly chopped and combined with garlic.

ACKNOWLEDGEMENTS

Marsha: I would like to send out a huge thanks to my husband, Don, who is, and has always been, a constant support in everything I pursue. His patience, thoughtfulness, and belief in this project over the last 12 months have been nothing but amazing. To my family, for enduring my questions and concoctions for the past year. To my sons, Willem and Miller, who never know what they are going to find in the refrigerator but take it all in stride. To my parents, Bill and Linda, for always answering questions about every single familial topic plus supplying much-needed ingredients, ideas, and support. And to Lori McCarthy, who pitched the perfect platform to showcase beautiful photography that has been in the darkroom for way too long.

Lori: I thank everyone who believed in me and pushed me to take all that I have collected and created and put it into this book. To Marsha Tulk, without whom this book would not have come to fruition; to the fishers, farmers, harvesters, and gatherers who love the land and sea beneath their feet. To those of you who accepted me into your homes, your sheds, and cabins, shared much tea, recipes. and stories—you inspired me to do this. I am grateful to you all. To my mom and dad, who always believe I am capable when I set my mind to something. To my children, Maria and Daniel: this book is for you. It is my hope that the bounty of this land will be here for you to enjoy and thrive on as you grow and discover all that it has to offer. Please take care of it—it's in your hands.

To the team at Boulder, specifically Stephanie Porter, Todd Manning, Tanya St. Amand, and Gavin Will, for believing in this project and for giving us so much influence in and support for how the finished project would look.

To Ritche Perez and Jonathan Randell Smith for their patience and skill in taking photographs of us together. They made an unfamiliar experience successful.

A special thanks to Quidi Vidi Brewery, Newfoundland Distillery Company, Newfoundland Salt Company, Alexis Templeton, John Templeton, Larry Hann, Brian Power, Brad Leyte, Laura Nesbit, Alex Blagdon, Vanessa Rideout, Bernard and Shelly, Mildred Knight (Nan Knight), Leonard Eddie, Chris Walsh, Shawn Dawson, Andrew McCarthy, Andrew Butler, Jason McCarthy, Jim and Regina McCarthy, Angie and Jeremiah Shea, Todd Newhook, Barb Hudson, Noel and Christina Brown, Jim and Roxy Hudson, Madeline Tulk, Clayton and Madeline Watkins, Geoff Tulk, Rod Stowe, Clarence Lucas, Eric Dodge, Jackie Skinner, John and Jane Green, and Rebecca and Bob Penton.

To those who contributed and stood by us on this journey, we thank you. Without all of you, this would not have been possible.

PHOTOGRAPH DETAIL AND CREDITS

Unless specified, all food photographs are by Marsha Tulk. Below photographer credits are in parentheses; all locations are on the island of Newfoundland.

Inside front cover collage (clockwise from top left): Willem Tulk, Don Tulk, and Bill Hudson, Flat Bay Brook (Norm Somerton); Quidi Vidi Battery (Marsha Tulk); Lori McCarthy, St. John's (unknown); Alex Hudson hauling wood, St. George's, c.1950 (Jim Hudson); fishing stage in Harbour La Cou, Harbour La Cou (Marsha Tulk); Nancy Hudson, Plum Point (Ron Delaney); Grey River (Marsha Tulk); Harold Tulk, Fischelles (unknown); Daniel McCarthy (Ritche Perez); Beachy Pond, Terra Nova National Park (Don Tulk); Three Brooks, Flat Bay Brook (Marsha Tulk); Jackie Skinner, St. George's.(Marsha Tulk).

Page iii   Mobile Beach (Marsha Tulk).
Page iv   Sunrise, Adies Lake (Marsha Tulk).
Page viii   Shore greens salad, Mobile Beach (Marsha Tulk).
Page x-xi   Middle Cove Beach (Marsha Tulk).

Author Forewords

Page xii   Marsha Tulk and Lori McCarthy, Southern Shore (Jonathan Rendell Smith).
Page xiii   Lori McCarthy (Victoria J. Polsoni).
Page xiv   Lori McCarthy with salt fish, St. Anthony (Victoria J. Polsoni); Lori McCarthy and Bill Butler, location unknown (unknown).
Page xv   Lori McCarthy ice fishing, Middle Gull Pond (Marsha Tulk).
Page xvi   Vanessa Kenny and Lori McCarthy, Middle Gull Pond (Ritche Perez).
                 Linda Hudson and Marsha Tulk in outfitters tent, Terra Nova National Park (Don Tulk).
Page xvii   Marsha Tulk, St. John's (Ritche Perez).
Page xxviii   Marsha Tulk salmon fishing, Flat Bay Brook (Don Tulk).
Page xix   Marsha Tulk, East Coast Trail (Don Tulk).
Page xx   Marsha Tulk and Lori McCarthy, Southern Shore (Jonathan Rendell Smith).

After the Long Haul

Page 1   Capelin on the rocks, Middle Cove Beach (Marsha Tulk).
Page 2   Percy Morris polishing lobster tin, St. George's, c.1940 (Jim Hudson).
Page 4   Capelin on the beach, Middle Cove Beach (Marsha Tulk).
Page 5   Miller Tulk casting net for capelin, Middle Cove Beach (Marsha Tulk); Cast net with capelin, Middle Cove Beach (Marsha Tulk).
Page 6   Jim Hudson with dip net, Middle Cove Beach, 1974 (Bill Hudson); Linda and Jim Hudson collecting capelin, Middle Cove Beach, 1974, (Bill Hudson); Willem, Miller, and Marsha Tulk at the capelin roll, 2005, Middle Cove Beach (Don Tulk).

Jiggs 'n' Reels

On the Hunt

Pantry to Plate

Inside back cover collage (clockwise from top left): Marsha Tulk, St. George's Bay (Don Tulk); Maria McCarthy (Ritche Perez); Miller and Willem Tulk, Fischelle's Beach (Marsha Tulk); Beachy Pond, Terra Nova National Park (Marsha Tulk); Marsha Tulk, Middle Cove (Marsha Tulk); Lori McCarthy and Marsha Tulk with QV beer, St. John's (Marsha Tulk); John Templeton and Lori McCarthy canning moose, St. John's (Marsha Tulk); Don Tulk, Markland. (Marsha Tulk); Matt Butler, location unknown, c.1950 (unknown); Pitcher plant, Beachy Pond, Terra Nova National Park (Marsha Tulk); Rose Blanche Lighthouse (Marsha Tulk); Don Tulk, Terra Nova National Park (Marsha Tulk); Lori McCarthy and Alex Blagdon, Fogo Island (Alex Blagdon); Ray Butt, St. George's, c. 1950 (Jim Hudson); capelin (Marsha Tulk).

INDEX

Lori McCarthy is a chef, forager, educator, advocate and passionate oudoorsperson dedicated to preserving and celebrating the cultural foods of Newfoundland and Labrador. Her core values embrace locally sourced regional cuisine and wild foods from the land and sea, reflected in the food experiences and workshops she offers through her company Cod Sounds and her work with the Livyers Cultural Alliance. Lori has been listed as a hidden gem in *National Geographic* and as offering one of the eight great excursions in North America by *Costal Living*.

Marsha Tulk grew up and married on the west coast of Newfoundland but raised her two boys on the east coast. She holds a Bachelor of Fine Arts (Visual) majoring in photography and printmaking and a Bachelor of Education (Secondary) from Memorial University of Newfoundland.

Sunset, Adies Lake

NFLD RANGERS